This is an authorized facsimile of the original book, and was produced in 1973 by microfilm-xerography by University Microfilms, A Xerox Company, Ann Arbor, Michigan, U.S.A.

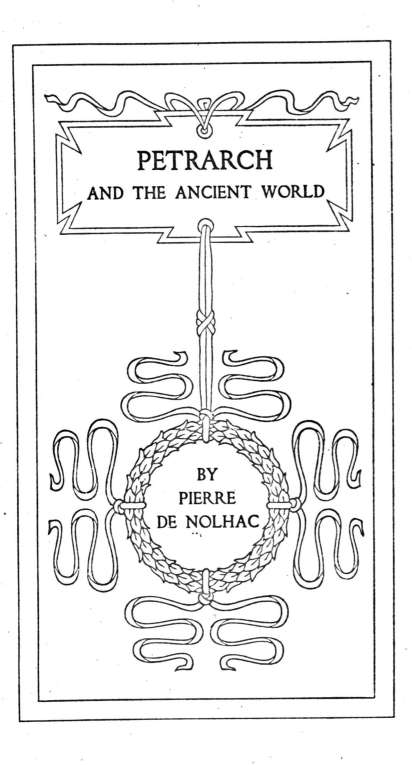

# PETRARCH
## AND THE ANCIENT WORLD

BY
PIERRE
DE NOLHAC

# THE HUMANISTS' LIBRARY

Edited by Lewis Einstein

III

# PETRARCH AND THE ANCIENT WORLD

# A TABLE OF CONTENTS

Preface                                                          ix
I. Petrarch as Initiator of the Renaissance        3
II. Petrarch's Library                                           43
III. Petrarch and his Masters
   Virgil                                                             97
   Cicero                                                            108

# PREFACE

# PREFACE

**\* \***

HREE years ago Italy summoned the scholars of the world to assist in the solemn celebration of the sixth centenary of the birth of Petrarch. On the twentieth of July, 1304, there was born at Arezzo a poet of Florentine parentage, whose works were to hold up to posterity one of the brightest mirrors of the Latin genius. Had his fourth and fifth centenaries been celebrated after our modern fashion, it is likely that the poet of Madonna Laura would alone have been the subject of all the speeches, poems, and commemorative inscriptions. It is due to the progress of scholarship in our time that Petrarch is honoured not only as a creator of Italian poetry, but as the apostle of the renaissance of letters throughout the whole of Europe, as the humanist and the scholar, as the poet and prose-writer, of the Latin tongue, which in his day was the universal speech of the cultivated world. It even seems as if by common consent the highest rank is accorded to the humanist in him, who revived once more the worship of the Ancient World. The work of modern criticism has resulted in vindicating such of

Preface  Petrarch's claims as his own contemporaries had clearly recognized.

This book attempts to throw light on one aspect of his historic rôle. A Latin writer of French nationality esteems himself honoured in having been asked to address a cultivated public on the other side of the Atlantic on the subject of one of the great ancestors of the Italian nation, to whom the entire thinking portion of mankind should render homage.

Palace of Versailles, July, 1907

# I
# PETRARCH AS INITIATOR OF
# THE RENAISSANCE

# I
## PETRARCH AS INITIATOR OF THE RENAISSANCE

**⁂**

HE Renaissance of letters in the fourteenth century had its source in the mind of a poet of genius living in the midst of a circle of friends, whom he had formed, taught, and inspired by his example, and fed by his thought. Never has the action of a single man proved more successful in preparing so powerful and fruitful a movement of the human intellect. The various researches of the last century concerning Petrarch's life and works all point to this conclusion.

Modern scholarship has thrust his national glory as an Italian poet into the background. It had long been dazzling, and its brilliance, reflected again and again in imitations of the Canzoniere, penetrated nearly all the other literatures of Europe. If Petrarch is still looked on to-day as the first of Italian lyric poets, no one now regards him as the rival of Dante. But as initiator of the Renaissance his fame keeps pace with our growing knowledge of the part he played therein. The singer of Laura hid the great humanist from the

3

eyes of our fathers. We have realized better than they the true meaning of the famous ceremony on the Capitol, and have come to understand that the poet of the Latin tongue, solemnly crowned by the Roman people on Easter Day, 1341, had other claims than love-verses to the admiration of his time. Indeed, he affected to care but little for his songs and sonnets. Trifles he called them, or experiments in the vulgar tongue (rerum nugellae meae vulgarium fragmenta). He was well aware that others could rival him in this field; and in spite of all that has been said to the contrary, he seems to have recognized without any jealousy the excellence of the Divina Commedia. To his mind his own mission was quite other; and he knew none more glorious. Petrarch was convinced that by his researches among ancient books, by his Latin poems, his historical and moral compilations, he was bringing back to the modern the glories of the antique world, forgotten or disfigured by the ignorance of ages. The credit of this part which he played with great deliberation and maintained with tireless energy through his long life, posterity now yields to him without contest, and greets in him no mere precursor, but an initiator of modern thought. And thus his fame has spread the more widely. The writer whom a single nation claimed takes rank amongst those who have contributed to our civilization of to-day, and to whom honour is due

4

from every people. Not only in the literary his- tory of Italy, writes Georg Voigt, but in that of the whole civilized world, nay, even in that of the development of the human mind, the name of Petrarch shines like a star of the first magnitude; nor would it seem less brilliant, had he never written a line in the Italian tongue.

2

Petrarch was the first modern man. No other phrase so well defines him. Individuality, the essential feature of the new man that Italy was fashioning, shines out in him with extraordinary vividness. By the direction of his thought he all but escaped from the influences of his age and his circle; and this assuredly is the most certain sign of his genius. It matters very little that his ideas are not original: his sentiments are, and this to an extraordinary degree. It was a poet, not a thinker, who was going to act upon the world and help its transformation.

Gifted even as a child with so fine a sense of beauty that the mere harmony of the Ciceronian phrase was enough to enchant him, he joined to his disdain of mediaeval literature an equal scorn of the studies which led to fame and fortune, the sciences which in his time were the basis of all intellectual education,—jurisprudence, theology, and scholastic philosophy. From the utilitarian path, in which all the influences about

him, at Avignon, Montpellier, and Bologna, urged
him to walk, he was turned by an extreme poetic sensibility, which all his life was to dominate
every other faculty. It was in the enthusiasm of
his first studies that he discovered his masters,—
the ancients. He wanted no others, because he
had taste for no others; and the circumstances of
his career, which freed him more and more from
material cares, put no hindrance in the way of
his choice. By imagination he was transported
into the world of his books; he lived the past life
of his race, where the pride and fire of his Italian
patriotism were fed:

> Gente di ferro e di valor armata,
> Siccome in Campidoglio al tempo antico
> Talora per Via Sacra o per Via Lata.

Step by step his education was perfected in that
ideal society which he reconstructed, first of all
for himself alone; and his mind was formed by
the writers he chose as guides. Thereby his personality doubtless loses in our eyes the relief maintained by Dante's, who had barely pierced the
shell of the antique world. But what appears ar-
tificial to us at a distance meant for his own generation a very striking and a very fruitful originality. It caused wonder, it aroused discussion,
and won erelong the admiration of all. If he had
not the encyclopaedic knowledge of a Vincent
de Beauvais or a Bacon, he presented to his own

day the example of a culture no less vast, and altogether new,—a culture of which his literary work is the exact reflection. At once a lyric and epic poet, historian, geographer, moralist, religious writer, controversialist, even orator, he reveals in himself something of the universal man, whom the following age was to know. To see him in this character more clearly, let us look at certain details. Petrarch was interested in art, and had some skill in drawing. He sang Provençal songs, or his own, in the vulgar tongue, accompanying himself on the lute. Outside his books a large number of practical things occupied his mind and roused his enthusiasm, from gardening to the theory of government. The full Renaissance—that of Leonardo and Michael Angelo—would show completer men; but even judged by this standard, he is to be counted among the most imposing figures of the great ages of Italy.

Having formed himself on antique models, Petrarch took up arms against the false science and the faulty methods of his day, sustained by a burning love of truth and by that scorn of common ignorance which is in itself a challenge. These were the two impulses, not equally noble, but in him equally strong, which inspired his long research and directed his polemics. Astrology reigned in the scientific world of his day. It was consulted by princes and taught in the universities. The Church tolerated it occasionally,

7

and at all events recognized its seriousness by condemning certain of its practices as the work of the devil. Magic also, on the strength of its long Oriental traditions, inspired general respect. Both astrologers and magicians found in Petrarch their enemy. By the aid of Cicero and Saint Augustine, but above all faithful to the clear general ideas with which the antique spirit had imbued him, he rose beyond such notions as the intervention of demons, and saw in the occult sciences only the fruit of human folly and malignity. He believed neither in horoscopes nor dreams; every research of the kind was to his mind quite other than dangerous: it was altogether foolish and sterile. It wanted no little courage to denounce the imposture of scholars and the credulity of the public, to ask if the one were the more odious or the other more absurd; and there was some merit in consenting to stand alone, or nearly so, in this opinion. For, indeed, Petrarch was very far from having the support of the sentiment of his time. At the most a voice here and there echoed his thought. Nay, even in the fifteenth century we shall see some part of the ground he conquered for rational science abandoned by the humanists themselves.

To this same contest, waged in the name of common sense, belong his attacks on medicine. At first he brought them under the notice of the pope in the form of letters. Then certain counter-

attacks on poetry, by the doctors of Avignon, gave him a subject for his pen which lasted his lifetime. He did not, however, deny the possibility of a science of medicine,—though he had his doubts if even the ancients possessed such; but the practitioners who claimed possession of it in his day had not established its method, and meanwhile were shamelessly exploiting the folly of their contemporaries. The details of this controversy are to be found in divers letters and four books of Invectives against a Doctor, which give us at the same time an insight into the writer's ideas on the natural sciences. Doubtless he had made no special study of these sciences; and in his mind they ranked too far below the study of man as a moral being; but at least we may say that he perceived their first principles. His experiments in scientific gardening, revealed by his notes, his observations on plant-life and the circumstances governing it, were one day to form the basis of botany. And in a neighbouring domain, did he not point with scorn and rage to the vanity of alchemic researches? Did he not emphatically thrust aside the bestiaries, the lapidaries, and all the legendary literature of the mediaeval naturalists, with which the Tesoro of Latini was still encumbered? Did he not part company even with Pliny and the ancients concerning certain fables they had handed down, which experience did not verify? This attitude

9

of Petrarch, which we take for granted to-day, was nevertheless not wanting in originality; and indirectly it served the cause of the experimental sciences which were to furnish the Renaissance with the field of its most lasting conquests.

With the charlatanism of leeches and alchemists he associated that of the lawyers. Their science, narrow and paltry, seemed to him to lack horizon; its sole end was greed and deception. Evidently he bore them a grudge for the rank assigned them in society, on the strength of an erudition vulgarly regarded as universal. With real zest he took up his pen to dispute with his old master, Giovanni d'Andrea, and convince him at least of his lack of literary culture. Fain would he see, he said, jurisprudence based on philosophy and eloquence. He had some vague knowledge of the great monuments of Roman law, and though incapable of gauging its full importance, was by no means ignorant of the work accomplished by the jurisconsults of Justinian. But the legal practice of his time made him sceptical of the value of law as a subject of instruction. One of his letters in reference to this sums up his opinion in a few words: "The science of law once fed by eloquence, fell first to the arid study of civil law and equity, till at last it sank to ignorance and babbling. The legislation of our fathers, a work of profound reflection and lucid genius, is misunderstood or betrayed. Justice, which they

served by the toil of their brains, is now a vile barter. They defended it; they armed it with sacred laws. To-day it is disarmed that it may be prostituted." According to him, a far higher rank should be given to the work of the orator and the moralist; and great would be the gain to science were it to dip once more into its first sources!

In the philosophic field the contest became a wider one. Petrarch treated the schoolmen of Paris no better than the decretalists of Bologna. He acknowledged dialectics to be an excellent tool,— "a step on which to mount;" but he waxed hot against those who would make the syllogism the very end of science, against those doctors, "blown up with nothingness," as he describes them, unworthy heirs of Saint Thomas and Master Albertus, disciples of Duns Scotus and the degenerate scholasticism. In one of the dialogues where he holds converse with Saint Augustine, he gives free rein to these sentiments: "The endless babble of the dialecticians swarms with confused definitions, the cause of everlasting disputes.... Ask any of this troop to define Man, or anything else you will, and he will always have an answer ready. But press him further, and he will keep silence; or perhaps, if the habit of magniloquence gives him boldness and a flow of words, his way of speaking will prove to you he has no true knowledge of the thing he has defined. I enjoy attacking persons so disdainfully careless and so frivolously curious. Why toil ever in vain, poor wretches, and strain your minds after empty subtleties? Why forget the reality of things and grow old among words? Why with white hair and wrinkled brow occupy yourselves still with childish things? And would to God your folly only hurt yourselves, that it did not too often ruin the noblest young intelligences!"

Against people so full of themselves, raillery is the surest weapon. Petrarch handled it again and again,—notably in a well-known passage where he describes the ridiculous fashion in which doctors' theses were sustained; and in the very dialogue I have been quoting from he claims with full confidence the saint's own words in his support. "I confess," he says, "that nothing more biting could be said against this scourge of serious study." Moreover, we must do our humanist the justice of owning that he never deceived himself by vague language, and that he had trained himself to seek for clear conceptions underlying words. But these were the mere externals, so to speak, of the philosophy of the time. If we go to the root of the matter, we shall see Petrarch attacking the principle of authority with a boldness no professional philosopher attained before him, and with a vigour of debate which has rarely been surpassed. True, he had read some pages of Abelard, but I do not think he owed anything in this respect to that great forerunner. Had he

not the real masters of his mind to teach him the The
method of personal research, which all around Initiator
him was forgotten and choked up? of the

The Averroists, very numerous in Italy, laid Renais-
claim to Aristotle no less than did the schoolmen; sance
and if Petrarch waged a fierce war with the former for their hostility to Christianity, he included
in the same large disdain the whole philosophy
of his age. It may be retorted, and with justice,
that his own was exceedingly incomplete, re-
duced, in fact, to nothing but ethics,—formed,
too, in the school of Cicero, and thus but a shadow of a shade. At least in his own day it was
his own, and no one shared it; and it was armed
with principles which were hewing new paths for
the mind of man. Somewhat uneasy at attacking
Aristotle, held up by the whole ancient world as
worthy of respect, he asserted first of all that the
only Aristotle known was disfigured by translations and commentaries. Besides, he says, what
matter the five syllables of this name sweet to
the ear of the vulgar, and this authority invoked
at every turn? "Of a truth I believe Aristotle was
a great and learned man; but after all he was
only a man. It was possible for him to be ignorant of some, nay, of many things. Moreover—
and why should we hide it?—Aristotle made mis-
takes, and this even in the most important matters." Such thoughts as these scattered through
Petrarch's works mark an epoch in the history

13

of ideas. It was no slight thing that Italy of the fourteenth century found a mind free enough to make a direct attack on the highest authority of the Middle Ages, "the master of those who know." It was as much the need of opposing another name to Aristotle's as the study of Cicero and of Saint Augustine that made Petrarch divine the importance of Plato. And not only did he oppose him at every turn to the Stagirite, but he proclaimed the marvellous sublimity and pre-excellence of his doctrine. True, this scorner of authority spoke almost entirely on the evidence of his masters, and the whole question remained somewhat vague in his mind; but there again he appears to have divined a whole new trend of modern thought, and he was the first to engage in the great Platonist battle which was to be contested in the fifteenth century.

This is not the place to explain how his ideas, so completely imbued with the spirit of free inquiry, were reconciled with his faith and his piety. But even this reconciliation is not so surprising, however alien to Renaissance practice it may seem at first sight. Our poet sought in philosophy only a means of becoming a better man; and for this he found a surer and completer means in the practice of the Christian life. Many bold spirits of the next age were to think like him. There is a certain eloquent prayer of Petrarch's, where the humanist gives way to the believer, where he

kneels "before the God of knowledge, preferring Him to all study and all instruction," —a prayer whose accent we shall find again on the lips of Marsilio Ficino and of Pico della Mirandola.

## 2

Petrarch ignored almost completely the science of his time, and in its place he substituted the pure study of antiquity. The men of the Middle Ages doubtless read and industriously transcribed the works of the pagans; but each of them knew but a few such, and not one altogether understood them. Even the writers of the greatest erudition—Albertano da Brescia, for instance—only heaped up quotations, often misplaced or travestied by the interpretation given them. The grammarians dug examples from the classics for technical instruction; the theologians or the philosophers borrowed texts for the support of a system. But the ancient spirit no man understood, and none even guessed its nature. Certain Italians, it is true, treasured with veneration the memory of the great writers of Rome, disguised in popular legend, and very vague even among the lettered. Brunetto Latini, who wrote in French, was among the instinctive scholars of antiquity. Dante, especially by the respect he showed the masters of Greece and Rome, most of whom were but names to him, seemed to recognize in them the educators of humanity. But they themselves were little in the pagans' debt. And what confusion and ignorance in Latini's or in Dante's vision of the past, and how incomplete their knowledge! Our poet had to be born before any lasting movement and any intelligent return to the ancients could take place. Italy, it must be owned, would have reached there without him; for at the heart of all mediaeval Italy lay an obscure craving after ancient thought. A country so deeply impregnated with classical tradition could not fail to find the lost path one day; but if from the history of the fourteenth century we can imagine the work and the action of Petrarch blotted out, we shall obtain some clear idea of the delay that would have ensued. No one since the time of the Fathers had so completely grasped the general classic Latin literature. He devoted the greater part of his time and fortune to gathering its fragments; and the broad outlines of the study and classification which he made from these have remained: we accept them still to-day. With a sure instinct which some of his successors lacked, he knew how to differentiate between the various authors, not praising antiquity in the mass, nor placing all the ancient writers in the same rank. A few of them he read and reread continually,—Virgil, Cicero, Horace, Livy, especially the first two, admiration for whom he declared had led to love, and with whom he felt his long study had made him more familiar than he could ever

16

have been with living men. It was the artistic The workmanship in ancient literature that fascinated Initiator him. Here for the first time for ages perfection of the of form decided the preferences of a scholar's Renais- mind. This search for the beautiful for its own sance sake, and this ranking of literary works in accordance with their greater or less revelation, were initiatives fraught with consequence. Moreover, they reëstablished literary criticism at the end of the Middle Ages, which had ignored it.

It is a satisfaction to assert the fact that this considerable contribution to erudition and to thought —the importance of which grows in our eyes the closer we study it—was accomplished in the name of aesthetic principles, and by a poet. Petrarch dreamed as a poet, and wrote as a poet, even when he believed his mission to be the restoration and reproduction in his own books of the knowledge of the ancients; and that alone was enough to keep him from being a pedant, even when he paid the greatest homage to pedantry. His wealth of imagination, his still greater wealth of sentiment, vivified his research, sustained his courage in the difficulties of study; it fired him with that ardour of activity and that continuity of effort which assured him success in the work he had planned.

The transformation of scientific thought, which was the essential work of the Renaissance, began in a renovation of form, born of the enthusiasm, entirely literary in its origin, that burned

17

in the heart of a poet of Italy. It was owing to the innermost character of his genius that he was the first of those "who loved dead letters with a living love, and found again in ancient dust the spark of eternal beauty."

Alongside the masterpieces Petrarch was fain to find a place for all the works of ancient Latinity, no matter of what kind, divining that the humblest débris of the edifice destroyed by the ages was of value in the reconstruction he had in his mind. He included therein the Fathers, who for him were the ancients of ecclesiastical literature; nor did he forget the Greek writers, then vanished from the West, of whose works he contrived to procure a few manuscripts and some rough translations. What disappointments did he meet in this search for books! What cries of indignation did he utter against the barbarian ages that had destroyed such vast treasures! "For every illustrious ancient name that I invoke, I call to mind a crime of the dark ages that followed!" he cried one day. "As if their own sterility had not been shame enough, they left the books born of the vigils of our fathers, and the fruits of their genius, to perish utterly. That epoch, which produced nothing, did not fear to squander the paternal heritage." He shook his contemporaries from their torpor, and recalled them to the duty imposed on them of saving the last remnants of a civilization full of great examples and fruitful in instruc-

tion. In words which reveal a full consciousness of his own mission, he cries, "I see myself standing on the border-line of two peoples, whence I survey at once the past and the coming race; and the plaint which our fathers did not utter, I shall at least sound in the ears of our children."

Books are the monuments which contain the most obvious deposit of ancient thought. It is necessary to first approach literature in order to save something of antiquity and to diffuse its knowledge. For this reason Petrarch multiplied copies of books, and every year enriched his library. He wished all his beloved ancients to "live under his roof," where they would be safe. He even thought of placing them after his death at the disposition of a select public, who would know how to preserve his collection and enrich it, who above all would seek in it for what he had found himself,—not merely a means of study, but recreation as well and the disinterested cultivation of the mind. Herein lies the conception of a modern public library. If the idea was never carried out, the honcur is none the less his of having conceived and suggested it to the fifteenth century, when it saw its earliest realization in Bessarion's gift to Saint Mark's of Venice.

But he was not so entirely absorbed by "the book" that he did not seriously consider what to-day we call archaeology. He makes no mention of the Roman monuments of Provence, disguised for him, I imagine, under mediaeval names; but in the journey to Rome, so long looked forward to, when he was thirty-two, the grandeur of the ruins, whose origins he could not mistake, made a profound impression upon him. "I feared that from books I might have conceived an exaggerated idea of Rome, and that I should be disenchanted when I saw it. On the contrary, it was once far greater, and to-day its ruins are far grander, than from my reading I had ever conceived." Thenceforward it was with a new force that he was able to call up in his imagination the age of the ancestors, and all the glorious past revealed to him in their own manner by historians. "It was our habit," he reminds a friend, "after having wandered through all the immense city, to go and rest from our fatigue at the Baths of Diocletian; and sometimes we used to climb upon the arches of that edifice, once so marvellous. The air is pure there; the view unhindered; and nowhere can one find more silence and sweet solitude.... Both in our walks inside the walls of the half-ruined city, and in our rests in that place, the piles of ruins were always before our eyes." Then he tells his delighted companion the tales of which the venerable stones were witnesses, adding to the memory of Brutus and the Camilli that of the saints and the first martyrs, endeavouring to name the hills, the temples, the porticoes, frequently accepting, but also sometimes correcting, the popu-

lar errors and the legends of the Mirabilia Urbis Romae. Let us, therefore, recognize in him one of the first scholars interested in the topography of the city of Rome; above all, let us greet him as the first poet whose meditations before these ruins were in the modern spirit.

But admiration of the ruins and the happiness he drew therefrom were not enough for Petrarch; he felt an anxious care as well for their preservation. To Paolo Annibaldi he wrote a letter in verse, begging him to restore, or at least to defend, the mutilated walls, which had resisted the barbarians, but which each day were crumbling more and more under the negligence of the popes and the shameful indifference of the inhabitants. "It will be an honour to you to have saved ruins which bear witness to the ancient splendour of inviolate Rome." Here he shows himself nearer us than many a humanist of the brilliant ages, who, full of enthusiasm as they were for ancient books and works of art, paid no attention to the remains of ancient buildings. He is more advanced even than Erasmus, who visited Rome three separate times, and lived long in Italy without making a single observation on an ancient monument.

His pious sentiments towards ruins were perhaps not more than patriotism or a poet's reverie. Nevertheless, they lift him above those princes, popes, and prelates, all of them great friends of art and letters, generous and sincere patrons, and

**The Initiator of the Renaissance** active promoters of the Renaissance, who none the less destroyed the Roman monuments, or left them to perish, without a single voice being raised to protest in Petrarch's indignant tone.

Nor was the curiosity of our humanist less keen on other points. During his stay in Rome he bought, he tells us, the medals which the peasants brought him, and with emotion deciphered on them the names of the emperors. Less zealous – but then also with less opportunity – than his friend Rienzi in collecting inscriptions, he went as far as to read them. He even quoted them, and declared himself to be an impassioned admirer of antique statues. In all this, doubtless, there is only a presentiment of the marvellous researches reserved for Italy in the fifteenth and sixteenth centuries. Flavio Biondo and Ciriaco d'Ancona were to leave far behind them Petrarch's confused ideas. But as a collector of manuscripts his zeal has never been surpassed; nor has the success of his discoveries, even in the time of Poggio and the Nicolli.

## 2

It was a memorable day for Petrarch, which for long he could never think of without tears, when, under the porch of the church of Saint Agricol at Avignon, he spoke with Niccola Rienzi of Rome's mission in the world. He believed he had found in him the man destined to raise the Republic out of its miseries, and to renew, in the

political world, its ancient splendour. For himself he reserved the task of bringing new life to the literary fame of their common mother, of taking up again the broken thread of Latin thought. Here the poet's rôle was less chimerical than the tribune's. When Rienzi fell halfway, a victim to his Livian political ideal, Petrarch, though sorely wounded, still went on his own road, and fulfilled the task he had imposed on himself. His work was straitly modelled on that of the antiquity he had brought to light. It lacked originality of form and often of matter; it paved the way for a whole imitative literature, which was to be as much a hindrance as an aid in the development of national letters. Nevertheless, this very imitation was a great step forward, and a novelty of the most far-reaching consequence. It contributed to the forming of vigorous generations, who, deliberately or not, were one day to place arts and letters at the service of a forgotten ideal.

The writings of Petrarch and those of Boccaccio, his disciple, helped first of all to preserve for Latin the character of literary language par excellence. Toward the end of his life Boccaccio repudiated his romances; and from the moment when he began to dream of his epic poetry, Petrarch attached no further importance to his "fragments in the vulgar," which had given him fame in his youth at the court of Avignon. The works on which these great men counted for winning glory are not read to-day. Nevertheless, their calculation was not so far out as it might seem; for the greater number of these works had an immense popularity."Whatever happens," cried Salutati, "one must recognize that Petrarch is superior to Cicero and Virgil;" and the good chancellor of Florence devoted many pages to the development of this opinion. The whole of his age thought as he did, and its literature was modelled on these vigorous writings in the Latin tongue which produced the illusion of genius. The exercise of such an influence on its own day gives to Petrarch's work in the history of letters a position analogous to that of beams in the support of buildings. Hidden from the eye, we never think of them; yet an examination of them is indispensable for a thorough understanding of the construction.

The search after artistic effect is easily perceivable in Petrarch's style. If in this respect he treated the two languages he used in the same fashion, in Latin he was assuredly the first stylist of modern times. He retouched and revised his books, filling with corrections the margins of his manuscripts in verse or prose. This we see in all the rough drafts which we possess in the poet's hand. The second version of his Life of Scipio reveals hundreds of retouches for the form alone, meant to add to the clearness of the text, or to give elegance and brevity to the phrase. The result is

here of less importance than the example af- forded by the effort. Moreover, call it mediocre, if you will, obscure, pompous, full of solecisms, faults of grammar, even barbarisms, the verse weighted by prosaic terms, and the prose confused by tags of poetry, none the less the Latin style of Petrarch has a character which makes it nearly always readable: it has originality. He had learnt that the style should be the man. He craves for his a personal accent, "as in the voice," and claims for every author the right to frame a language for himself. This was the death-blow to the monotonous Latin of the Middle Ages, which even Dante himself never dreamt of liberating from the severe logic that barred from it all free fancy. With Petrarch individual feeling, passion and colour invaded the scholastic tongue and transformed it. To this emancipation we owe the Latin of Poggio, of Politian, and of Erasmus.

Most of the artistic forms cultivated in the vast literature of humanism have their beginnings more or less directly in Petrarch. If the Latin epic was henceforth fed from a Virgilian source, it is because Petrarch dipped there for his Africa. The familiar epistle in verse, descriptive or moral, modelled on Horace, he handed on to Filelfo, ready for the expression of modern feelings. The bucolic allegory, inherited though it was from the past, had less success; Petrarch and his immediate successors were the last representatives of a vanishing form of literature. On the other hand, after them begins the great lyrical and elegiac output, forms at which they barely tried their hand. But in compensation new life was given to the prose epistle by the Familiares and Seniles collections. These, with their intimate personal chronicle, their political studies, their learned and moral dissertations, were destined to flourish, to develop more and more every day. Nor was his example of collecting and preparing his correspondence for the public to be lost. Henceforth it became a part of every humanist's duty to leave to posterity a witness, sometimes precious and often insignificant, of his studies and his friendships.

Historical composition occupied a large place in the work of Petrarch. Though he made a great effort to consult as many sources as possible, and to verify these, though he had every intention of employing a critical method, he worked rather as a moralist than as a historian. An enthusiastic student of personality, his first interest is always in the tale of the actions of great men. Now he conceives history as a collection of portraits and anecdotes (Res Memorandae), now as biography (De Viris illustribus), two forms which in the literature of the Renaissance were to have an equal success. The great part which biography especially was to play is well known. It was closely allied to the imitation of Petrarch and Boccaccio, the one inspired by the other, and likewise to the

development of the idea of Glory, to which they were the largest contributors.

As historian our poet has one particular merit. To his earliest De Viris is due the first application of modern intelligence to the legends of the ancient East, an experiment doubtless very uncertain, sometimes even puerile in his hands, and much confused by Latin traditions, but not unworthy of some attention when one considers how slender was the information at the disposition of the writer. On Roman ground his steps were more assured; and it is not too much to say that he rediscovered the sources of the history of Rome. In giving back to Livy his due fame,—Livy whom he looked upon as the chief national historian,—above all, in reading him and using his matter with intelligence, Petrarch prepared the way for a great number of important works. Although from various reasons—his spirit of independence, for instance, or his disdain for his own time—he declined in nearly every case to chronicle contemporary events, other reasons drove his successors in a contrary direction; but the method of research, the tone of the narrative, the exact measure of the imitation of the ancients, had already been settled by Petrarch; and the historiography of Humanism begins with him.

The dialogue De Contemptu Mundi (Secretum), where he makes most intimate confession of his aspirations and his weaknesses, was without imi-

tators, for no other humanist shared the lofty and
the restless mind of Petrarch. But the moral treatises (De remediis utriusque fortunae, and De vita
solitaria, &c.) were repeated time after time, and
under various forms. We shall see the moral dissertation reappear applied to every subject. The
matter of it is always more or less directly borrowed from the ancients, while it is studded with
quotations from their works, the author "begging
from door to door" the testimony of poets and
prose writers. Of that form, it is true, where Petrarch, in spite of his abuse of the thought of other
men, put the whole of himself, revealing his
heart at every instant, we shall only see more or
less adroit developments, where words take the
place of ideas, and where nothing is so much lacking as sincerity. One treatise, the De ignorantia,
of great importance on account of some of the
questions it raises, is an early type of the higher
philosophical controversy. The Itinerarium Syria-
cum, outcome of the author's taste for travelling
and his geographical studies, marks a date in the
near restoration of such studies, more especially
by its attempt to apply ancient texts and names
to modern localities. Even the heated polemical
tract, which the humanists lamentably abused, is
foreshadowed in Petrarch's Invectivae contra me-
dicum quemdam, in the Epistolae sine titulo, and
the Apologia contra Gallum. His imitators could
only add filth and personal calumny; for already

he had contributed the irritability of the man of letters and the blindness of the partisan.

Of one important branch of the literary labour of the fifteenth century, the translation of Greek, Petrarch was incapable. Nevertheless, here also he was the creator. Did he not obtain from a Calabrian, a literal interpretation of the Iliad and the Odyssey, having the work carried out at his expense? Indeed, he all but divined the importance of that mysterious literature of the masters of Rome, completely unknown in the West. The Greek lessons he took at Avignon from the monk Barlaam were the first ever received by any humanist. And if he never acquired any grasp of the language, at least he desired to taste the most venerable of the work it had produced. The translation, which he had carried out along with Bocaccio, however chaotic it may seem to us, revealed to these two precursors of Hellenism, and made known to the first generations of the Renaissance, the poetic world of Homer. An activity so varied and so wide explains the influence exercised by Petrarch on his contemporaries. None before him had ever received such homage. The Roman barons forgot for a moment their fierce quarrels, to celebrate with antique ceremonial his triumph on the Capitol. Princes esteemed themselves honoured in having him under their roof. An old, blind schoolmaster travelled all through Italy on foot, led by two youths, to meet Petrarch, to embrace his knees, and to kiss the brow under which was born such wealth of lofty thoughts. For several generations after his death the humanists had a kind of cult for him. We know the story of Leonardo Bruni. When little more than a boy, during the Tuscan civil wars, he was shut up in a fortress where there was a portrait of the poet. The sight of this venerated picture, and the meditations suggested thereby, sufficed, it seems, to fire in him a passion for letters, and decided his vocation. So in other days had the painting of some saint, on a church wall, inspired a youth with the desire for the cloister.

## 2

It is not in the revival of art that Petrarch's hand can be traced in the Renaissance. Yet one may hazard the guess that he did not remain indifferent to the great movement which was being carried forward by his side. He collected drawings, searched for miniatures, and kept among his treasures that Madonna of Giotto, whose beauty, he said in his Testament, was hidden from the ignorant and delighted the masters of art. He loved artists, and frequented their company. If he does not speak of the painters of Giotto's school, and if he seems to know nothing of their work, at least in his youth he had known Giotto. Much later the Paduan artists who painted for the Carrari palace the portraits of illustrious men worked according

to his counsels. So had Simone Martini done at Avignon; and to please the poet he had attempted to represent Romans in a costume different from that of the fourteenth century. One can hardly be certain here of a personal influence. Nevertheless, these first attempts at symbolism in the antique manner, which we find in the frescoes of the time and in the decoration of books, evidently owe something to the intellectual changes brought about by Petrarch and his disciples. In his Africa he filled the description of the palace of Syphax with mythological attributes and subjects of which the mediaeval world knew nothing. He has no credit for the illustrations of his Trionfi, which were repeated, again and again in the fifteenth and sixteenth centuries, in paintings, bas-reliefs and tapestries. But it is only natural to suppose that the frontispiece of the manuscripts of the Viris Illustribus were inspired by the author. The noble figure of Glory on her chariot, distributing crowns, is without doubt among those new types to which artists would give definite shape, but which were first born in a poet's brain. In the fourteenth century, however, literature and the arts had not yet drawn near to one another. Even in the mind of Petrarch they remain apart. Indeed, he has nothing to say on the architecture or the decorative arts of his time; not one allusion to the marvellous religious and civil monuments which were being begun, or completed,

31

or embellished under his eyes. One feels that this Florentine, son of an exile, who never longed to return to Florence, lived, just for that reason, outside the most active centre of Italian art. So far as sculpture is concerned, his feeling for human beauty gave him an exceedingly correct aesthetic theory. For example, he distinguishes rigidly between the value of a work of art and the riches of its material. But one would like to find some more precise declaration, some proof of active sympathy with the efforts of the Pisan masters, whose work – if only the door of the Baptistery of Florence – cannot have been entirely unknown to him. His indifference makes one suspect he would not have appreciated or encouraged an Andrea Pisano. He was inclined to place the sculptors of his time far below the painters. "I have known some of them," he says, "but they were of less renown (than Giotto and Martini); for in this art our age is quite inferior."

But at least he did his part in restoring fame to works that for long had been despised. Indeed, he is perhaps the first writer who speaks of ancient art with admiration. An important equestrian statue, the bronze (no longer existing) of Marcus Aurelius at Pavia, is described by him in a letter to Boccaccio, in the style of an enthusiastic connoisseur. He saw at Rome – and twice, in verse and prose, he sang the praises of it – the celebrated Horse-tamers of the Quirinal, which he attributed to

Pheidias and Praxiteles. He was interested in the busts and statues of the emperors, as also in the inscriptions on them, which he had met with in Italy and seen scattered about Southern France. One fact seems specially conclusive. The most ancient Italian medals struck in the antique method, and belonging to a much earlier date than Pisanello's experiments, represent the lords of Carrara; and they were made in that very town of Padua where Petrarch died, surrounded by particular veneration. The Roman coins collected by him, and the noble designs of which he often praised so highly, can hardly be left out of count in the first attempt at the restoration of a lost art. The Initiator of the Renaissance

Art was indirectly concerned with certain novel sides of Petrarch's literary activity. It would not be easy to say to whom is due the credit of having revealed nature and landscape to the modern world. The Divine Comedy is full of descriptive tercets of incomparable force; but Dante's brief glimpses, flashed out for the most part in comparisons, could not have such an influence on literature as Petrarch's altogether conscious and elaborate passages of natural description. Those he inserted in his Latin works helped more than anything else to spread the feeling for nature in the books of the next generation. He was the first to look at a landscape and to try to render it visible in words, to seize the features of a place that spoke to his heart as would those of one he loved.

This art, which Aeneas Sylvius and others rediscovered in the fifteenth century, and which, very
much later, modern writers developed so highly,
seems already at its full maturity in Petrarch's
Latin. Call to mind, among a host of others, those
exquisite descriptions of the Fountain of Vaucluse, in prose and verse, the climbing of Mont
Ventoux, the women of Cologne bathing in the
Rhine, the rustic labourers in the fields of Capra-
nica, the outlook over the Lombard plain from the
height of St. Colomba, and—in a quite different
strain—the group of memory pictures by which
he recounted the voyage of an ancient fleet along
the Genoese Riviera.

Besides an accurate eye, he had a special love
for the picturesque, such as has ever since been in
vogue, and with which antiquity could not have
inspired him. He felt the poverty of the wild, of
rocky places, of forests and mountains, and gave
himself up to it with enchantment. It was a gran-
diose spectacle of nature that moved him so for-
cibly as to change the direction of his studies and
even of his conduct. Something even subtler entered into his love of travel. He roamed the world
with the tales of history in his mind. He knew
the mysterious charm with which the past has enveloped certain countries. Before Petrarch none
had expressed that entirely modern sentiment,—
historic emotion before sites or in cities that have
witnessed great events. This emotion, made up

as it is of memories, is generally all the deeper the more it is fed by study; and it is never really articulate save in such as, like him, are saturated both by poetry and erudition. Nor is there less originality in his psychological observations. Doubtless he owed much to Seneca and to the Fathers; but just as, in precise phrase, he painted the outward sights that attracted his eyes, so did he train his pen to render as exact an account of his moral being. In one of his letters, Ad posteros, he tells us the colour of his complexion, the variations of his vision, and more especially the aptitudes and qualities he recognized in himself. That alone justifies the assertion that autobiography in the full sense of the word began with him, and marks him out as a precursor of Montaigne.

The reading of all the various letters and treatises in which he studies himself, and hands himself over for our examination, is less fascinating than one might expect, burdened as they are with quotations and irrelevant reminiscences. But there is one book readable from end to end. Its sincerity is incontestable and its tone more deeply emotional than can be found elsewhere in his work. I mean the dialogues with Saint Augustine, which the poet called his Secret, and which are in very truth the intimate confessions of his heart and his genius. The questions of the saint probe pitilessly into the conscience of the believer, who answers, defending or accusing himself, with a

touching simplicity, owning both to the passions
in which man takes pride, such as love of glory,
and to the faults that cost dearest to avow, the
petty meannesses of vanity. Since Saint Augustine's, which inspired it, no book has so intimate-
ly revealed a soul; and, happily, that soul was
one of the most delicate and complex that ever
breathed.

の

Moreover, the Renaissance owes to Petrarch an
influence on manners. Among the ideas which
the poet spread most zealously is one which was
enough by itself to transform the entire moral
atmosphere,—that of glory. It had stirred within
the minds of certain mediaeval writers, but till
Petrarch it had never been the moving force of
any one's life, and no one had even thought out
a precise conception of it. Antiquity furnished
the theory, under a thousand forms, as well as
the most striking examples. History enabled him
to put his finger on the marks left by great spirits
and great masterpieces upon the earth. He in his
turn would win a place among those illustrious
ones, whom he felt were by his side, in spite of
the separation of the ages, and who never ceased
to belong, in some sense, to living humanity. He
is in quest of Fame,

Che trae l'uom di sepolcro e'n vita il serva.

Glory was the pilot of his conduct. "It is glory

which is the end of my labours," he cries at every
instant. "From my childhood I have desired above
all else the immortality of my name." His continual play of words upon the names of Laura
and the laurel is not merely a symbol of his two-
fold passion: it is the symbol of an obsession,
morbid at times, but whose very excess has in it
a generative force. He took endless pains to inspire the men about him with this desire for fame
which the ancients had taught him. He com-
mended it to his friends, his disciples, to princes,
even to popes. He preached it in all his books;
became its propagator, and almost its apostle. It
was he, not Dante, who clearly saw "come l'uom
s'eterna," and who flashed the vision on his age.
Henceforward there was a new mainspring of
individual effort within every man's reach. In
substituting for the Christian and certainly purer
ideal of the Middle Ages models that had passed
out of men's minds until he came, Petrarch became the master of fifteenth-century Italy. It was
first Livy, and then Plutarch, that formed the
characters of several generations. Ancient history
passed by an easy transition from the study to the
forum and the camp. Tyrants modelled themselves on Caesar, and the condottieri not infre-
quently on Scipio. In that Italy of the near future,
whose earliest types were already to be seen
around him in his friends the Correggi, the Carrari, even the Visconti, he assigned to the profes-

sional man of letters a social part. First and fore-
most, he was to be the dispenser of fame.

By the eulogies at its disposal, poetry can satisfy better even than the plastic arts that desire
for immortality which was to inspire the future
statesman and the soldier. The first honour should
be reserved, of course, for the distributer of praise,
the favourite of the Muses, worthy of sharing, as
Petrarch did himself, the laurel of the conquerors.
In ordinary life the humanist was to be the coun-
sellor of the prince or the republic; was to hold the
pen, or speak the word, in their name; and such
tasks fell to him by reason of his acquaintance
with the ancient world and his skill in elegant
phrase. Petrarch might have occupied such a place
in his day, might have solicited such burdens, if
on the one hand his love for solitude had been
less sincere, and on the other if the princes of his
time, who admired his eloquence, had had an
equal confidence in his judgement to justify their
employing him seriously in their affairs.

A subtle form of human activity retook possession of the world with Petrarch,—literature. The
didactic works of the Middle Ages, the compositions in the vulgar tongue of certain mediaeval
poetic centres, and the powerful efforts of isolated
genius, bear but a faint resemblance to the literary productions of modern times. In this respect,
from the fourteenth century onward, we moderns
feel more at home. A large cultivated public was

forming, and books found a wide circulation. For the first time we can watch, too, rivalries of different schools, coterie enthusiasms, the desire for
success, the play of petty vanities, and the impulse of loyal camaraderie. The appearance and
the development of all this are due to Petrarch
and his friends. He was the first man of letters,
and he lived and moved in a society made after
his own image. These, however, are but the mere
trivial aspects of a rôle which must also be regarded from a higher point of view. By his Latin
conversations with the learned of every country, especially those of France and Germany,
by circulating throughout the whole of wonder-
ing Europe his letters, poems, and treatises, he
formed a new bond between the western nations.
Once allied by a kindred theology, now they
were bound together by philosophy and literature. In a Europe still subject to ecclesiastical and
feudal authority, he founded a new power, outside Church and outside State, altogether moral,
altogether modern, the Republic of Letters. (Car-
ducci, Discourse at the Tomb of Petrarch.)

Finally he brought about a reform in the education of youth which it is impossible to ignore.
It was inevitable that after him the young generations should be brought up in the school of
the ancients. Great Italians like Guarino da Verona and Vittorino da Feltre, who had fed on his
books, would sketch out the new theory and try

The Initiator of the Renaissance

the first experiments. Out of humanism the humanities were to rise. And when they flourished in other countries, in the sixteenth century, Erasmus, Vivés, Budaeus, and Melancthon were in certain respects but the continuers of Petrarch. Detail, form, didactic method, many important things, remained for later discovery; he only cast into circulation general ideas. He was ill endowed for systematizing them, still worse for applying them to others than himself. But he clearly showed in antiquity the source of a vast educational theory, both literary and moral, from which henceforward every one could draw. And thus Petrarch is of the little band of spirits to whom we all of us owe something of our intellectual life. In measuring him we must not consider his knowledge, limited and insufficient on so many points, but rather judge his greatness by that of the ideas he served. In spite of the lapse of centuries Europe has not yet ceased to feed its thought on his period.

# II
# PETRARCH'S LIBRARY

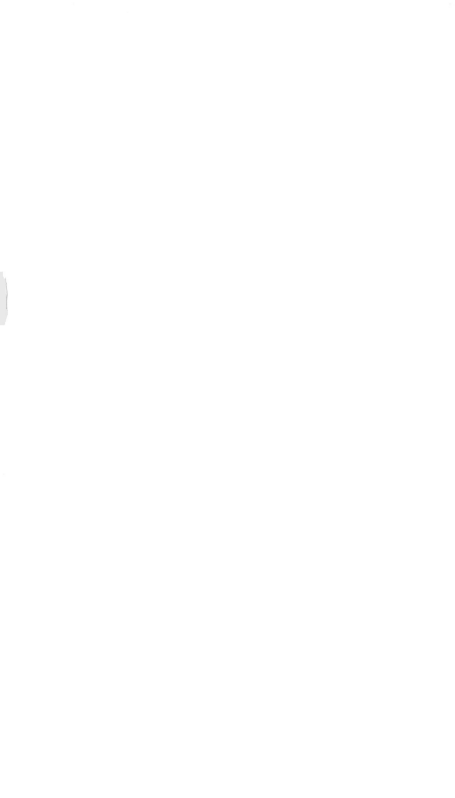

# PETRARCH'S LIBRARY

* *
*

OOKS first revealed the Ancient World to Petrarch. The history of his library, if we could have it complete, would be also the history of his mind. No one more than he has lived on books and for books. This poet, who conceived in a modern tongue such fair antique forms, devoted to the study of the ancients the best of his intellectual force. This Italian, so directly connected with the social activity of his time, chose for the domain of his thought a far remote past where he found the model of nearly all his individual production and the food of his morality. Every new book, every bibliographic discovery, every acquisition of an unknown work, left its mark on him, and gave a new spur to his mind. An anecdote of his early days shows him already given over to his favourite passion. When he was at Montpellier studying law, in obedience to his father's wish, but with his mind more full of literature than of anything else, he collected in his student's cabinet the works of the first masters he had chosen for himself, sacrificing to this all other pleasures.

He possessed Cicero, Virgil, and some Latin poets. His father paid him a surprise visit. "Fearing
such an event, I had hidden my treasures; and
now they were seized under my very eyes, and
thrown into the fire as if they had been heretical
books. I cried aloud as if I had been thrown in
myself; and then my father, I remember, seeing
my tears, drew out from the flames two black-
ened volumes, and holding out Cicero's Rhetoric
in one hand and Virgil in the other, 'Keep this,'
he said with a smile, 'to amuse you from time to
time; and Cicero for the study of civil law.' And
their company, few in number but noble, consoled me." Yet Petrarch's father was no enemy
of letters. If in this case he seems somewhat severe, and absorbed solely with the idea of his
son's success in the career to which he had forced
him, he had nevertheless done much to develop
in him the taste for study. He was himself an
admirer of Cicero and possessed a volume of his
works, the Delights, through which young Petrarch first made his acquaintance. "While still a
child," he wrote, "I gave myself up to the study
of Cicero, as much by natural instinct as by the
advice of my father, who held him in great veneration. My father might have easily developed
his own mind, had not material cares forced him,
an exile and burdened with a family, to devote
his noble intelligence to other duties." The modest and sympathetic figure of the Florentine

44

notary deserves to be pictured just as the poet saw it when he spoke of his youth to the friends of his old age.

The time spent in the study of law at Montpellier and Bologna was looked on by Petrarch as wasted. Once master of his own actions, and back in Avignon, he had no thought save for ancient books and poetry. The most precious object in the paternal heritage was the manuscript of Cicero which had initiated his childhood into the beauty of the Latin tongue. With the first money at his disposal he bought a fine copy of The City of God, sold at Avignon on the death of a bishop. Already he had in his possession Virgil, Servius, the Achilleiad of Statius, and some odes of Horace collected in a magnificent volume, the margins of which he filled later with notes and references to his reading. To add to this beginning of a collection he made the acquaintance of all the bibliophiles of the papal court. The presence of the pope on the banks of the Rhone gathered an international society in Avignon which made it the real centre of Europe, and gave rise to a considerable intellectual movement. But if the Curia was more intelligent and more friendly to letters than Petrarch would have us believe, still it was not so in the sense the young man desired. It is hardly likely that he could take advantage of the palace library. Though John XXII did much to enrich it, the collection was only open to those belonging to the Curia; and besides, he would have found but little there to add to his knowledge of the pagan writers, which were alone the object of his search. In the ecclesiastical and legal world of Avignon, where the struggle of ambition and "lucrative studies" played so great a part, he must have found but a faint echo of his own disinterested enthusiasm, reserved entirely for fine literature. Churchmen with a sincere love of literature being so rare, he appreciated the more those like Cardinal Colonna and his nephew Jacopo Colonna, the beloved Bishop of Lombez. And he deemed himself happy in the acquaintance of an old Italian jurisconsult, Raimondo Soranzo, who had collected in his library a great many books of the ancients. True, the old man hardly read any of these save law-books and the histories of Livy; but as Petrarch, in spite of his youth, was more learned than he on questions of antiquity, and helped him many a time in the interpretation of his favourite author, Soranzo conceived a friendship for him, treated him as a son, and let him use his library freely, lending him, and even presenting him with books. It was about this time that our poet took on himself voluntarily the work of copyist, transcribing for his own use the books that fell into his hands. He was at the outset of his career, without great resources, for no ecclesiastical benefices had yet fallen to him. He could neither buy nor have copies made

of all he wished to own. His pen helped him to his end with economy; and in compensation for his trouble, he grasped more thoroughly the meaning of the text, and obtained at the same time a copy of it for himself.

Petrarch's travels in his youth gave him opportunity for useful researches. In Paris, which he declared to be "the nurse of study in his time," he found a new atmosphere and a singular intellectual activity. The Italian and French scholars of the university, with whom he made friends, showed him their collections, and went with him to the book-shops. The ecclesiastic Dionigio da Borgo San Sepolcro gave him Saint Augustine's Confessions, not to enrich his mind, it is true, but rather as a remedy against the passions of his youth. Roberto de' Bardi, chancellor of Notre Dame, doubtless introduced him to the Library of the Sorbonne, recently reorganized, where foreigners were admitted. About the same time, another great bibliophile whom Petrarch knew personally, Richard de Bury, paid several visits to the capital of Philip VI; and in gratitude for the studious joys he had found there, called Paris the "paradise of the world." "So much did I love that city," he adds, "that my stay there seemed always too short. There are libraries pleasanter than scented chambers; there is a green orchard, hanging with every kind of book. There I opened my purse, I undid the strings, and threw my money about with a glad heart, to rescue the priceless volumes from filth and dust." Petrarch must have felt the same. If, unlike the Bishop of Durham, he would not choke down the memory of it, and preferred to paint Paris especially as "the city of disputes, with its cackling Rue du Fouarre," we must probably look for the reason in his hostility to France, and his perpetual slandering of that country caused by his sentimental politics.

He took his way through the northern provinces of the kingdom, which were not yet ravaged by war, and through Flanders. He made long journeys on horseback, preferring to go apart from his travelling companions, to meditate or to read in one of the books which never left him. But his special curiosity was always awake. He had learned already by experience that in convents there were chances of finding unknown books. And so, along the road, at the sight of an ancient-looking monastery, he would say, "Who knows if it may not contain something I should like." Then he turned aside, leaving the rest of the cavalcade, and knocked at the library door. He seems never to have met with books in as piteous a state as those which Boccaccio described so lamentably to his friends. Neither does he seem to have ever been badly received in a convent; and, always very friendly to monks, he does not impute to them that pride of ignorance and pedantic folly with which he so bitterly reproached

the clerical society of his time. He was grateful for the neglected treasures piously preserved by them for the satisfaction of his humanist curiosity. More than once he owed to them works which were new to him; and in the course of his travels they gave him information concerning the towns where there were libraries to visit. "I learned," he says, "on my arrival at Liège of the existence there of a fine collection of books; and I kept my companions till I had got copies of two discourses of Cicero. One was transcribed by a friend; the other, which I have since circulated in Italy, I made with my own hand. And for your amusement I will tell you that in that good barbarous town we had endless trouble to get a little ink, and when we got it, it was like saffron."

From certain notes taken on the first journey to Rome some years later, in 1337, we learn more of Petrarch's habits. Hardly had he been there a day or two; hardly had he paid his tribute of emotion to the city of his dreams, when we find him book-hunting. On March sixth, he had already made an acquisition; on the sixteenth another; and he carefully noted the dates on the covers of the volumes. They were works of piety, such as he had then no great mind to read; but the beauty of the copies tempted him. From the evidence of such purchases we may be sure he added to them, when he could, many a secular work. They were a heavy load to take back. The road was long; and such

baggage was troublesome to a traveller, whether
he went on horseback or crossed the Tyrrhenian
Sea. But the young bibliophile took such troubles
in good part, only too proud to be able to inscribe
on his books the glorious words "Romae emptus."

The chief motive of Petrarch's installation at
Vaucluse was his desire to work in peace, far from
the distraction of the town and from intruders,
and to hold with his books the long conversations
which he so charmingly described. He loved solitude passionately, provided always that he found
at his side, to quote the words of the French Ron-
sard, who was his close imitator,

Ces bons hostes muets qui ne faschent jamais.

He himself has described that same friendship
of books in the happiest fashion, in an epistle in
verse. "These are mysterious companions which
the ages have brought to me from every country,
illustrious by their language, by their genius, by
the works of war or peace. They are not exacting; a corner of a little house is lodging enough
for them; they obey all my orders; are always
there, and never weary me. They depart at my
desire, and return at my first call." In his many
descriptions of Vaucluse, which throw such clear
light on his rustic life, he hardly ever omits to
note some memory of his favourite occupation.
"Here is my life," he writes to a friend. "I get up
about midnight, and when dawn comes I go out.

But in the open, as inside the house, I study, I meditate, I read and write. Every day I visit the bare
mountains, the green valleys and the grottoes.
I wander by both banks of the Sorgue by myself, without meeting any one on my way, and in
company only of my own cares, which day by
day, moreover, grow less acute. . . . Here I have
made my Rome, my Athens, my fatherland. All
the friends I have, or have had,—not only those
whom I have seen and who have shared my life,
but men, too, who lived ages ago, and who are
only known to me through books, men whose acts
and characters, whose life and manners, whose
language and genius, I admire,—I gather often in
this narrow valley, and am more eager for their
conversation than for that of the crowds of crea-
tures who think they live because, when it is cold,
something floats from their lips which they take
to be the breath of life. So I wander, free and at
peace, as often as may be alone with my good
comrades."

To the ancients, whose works and memories
were about him in his retreat, he lent sentiments
and words. "I have retired to my transalpine
Helicon," he writes to the owner of a manuscript.
"Your Cicero has come with me. He is astounded
at the striking beauty of the place, and owns that
never in his estate at Arpinum was he—to use his
own words—surrounded by more delicious cool
streams than here with me by the Sorgue. . . . And

indeed he seems to enjoy himself and to be my willing guest. We have passed ten days of peaceful leisure together in this place, the only one outside Italy where I can freely breathe." What wonder if living in so close an intimacy with men of the past, he thought of making their history the chief object of his studies? His poem of Africa, written in honour of Scipio Africanus, and the De Viris illustribus were the natural outcome of his reading at Vaucluse. Of all his works these two reflect most nearly his entirely Roman culture.

Petrarch showered tender words on books. His library was "his daughter," "the only balm of his sorrows" (Bibliothecae meae quam in filiam adoptavi. . . . Libellos in quibus mihi omnis ferme laborum quis et solatium vitae est). He asked health from it when he was ill. On one of his journeys in Italy a fever kept him prisoner at Bologna. Tortured by insomnia and unable to write a line, he nursed himself back to health by reading. From his own description we see him searching in the heap of books with which his bed was littered for the one that contained De finibus. This occupation became indispensable to life. One day a very intimate friend, anxious at seeing him so overdriven at the task of writing the Africa, which he had undertaken with his ordinary fierce zeal, wanted to surprise him into breaking off his research. "He came on me suddenly," says Petrarch, "and begged me to do him a favour, which would be

very pleasant to him and very easy to me. I con-
sented trustingly, for I could refuse him nothing,
and sure of his having no desires for me other
than those of an excellent friend. 'Give me the
keys of your cupboard,' he said. I was much surprised, but I gave them. Thereupon he took away
my books and all my writing materials, and locked
them up carefully. As he was leaving me he said,
'I order you ten days' holiday; and during that
time, according to our bargain, I forbid you to
read or write.' Then I understood the trick he had
played me. He thought I should be simply resting; but I felt as if he had taken away part of myself. The day passed more slowly than a weary
year. Next day I had a headache from morning
to night. The third had hardly begun when I felt
already a touch of fever. My friend heard of it,
returned, and gave me back my keys. I was cured
at once, and seeing that work was, as he said, my
food, he never asked such a thing again." And all
to whom study has grown to be the most impe-
rious necessity must see themselves reflected in
Petrarch.

At Vaucluse there were a good many books, and
the masters' studies on these allow us to know
their nature. "Veterum ingenia quorum copia
magna est.... Librorum copia ingens adest fide-
liumque convictus atque obsequium amicorum.
Versaberis cum sanctis, cum philosophis, cum
poetis, cum oratoribus, cum historicis." The col-

lection was formed solely according to his taste and his special intellectual interests. There were none of the mediaeval works which had been the joy of the cultivated men of Avignon. The futilities of these, glanced at one morning by the poet, were enough, he tells us, to take the taste out of all his other reading that day. The pope's library, of which he had the run,—indeed, he had been asked to arrange the Ciceronian manuscripts in it,—excited in him no envy; the law-books and the works of the schoolmen which encumbered it seemed to him but a sterile possession.

If he desired books round him, it was that he might read them and feed his mind on them. "There are persons," said he, "who accumulate books as they would any other objects whatsoever, not for use, but for the mere pleasure of collecting, to adorn their house and not their mind." The case of the scholar Sammonicus, who possessed seventy thousand volumes, filled him rather with fear than admiration. How had he ever time even to read the titles and look at their outsides! "A fine art that in truth, which turns a philosopher into the keeper of a book-shop!" The number of books is of little importance. "To get glory from them it is not enough to own them; you must know them, place them not on your library-shelves, but in your memory, lodge them not in a bookcase, but in your brain. Otherwise you will be always something less than the shop-

man who sells them, or even than the cabinet that holds them." Petrarch's friends shared his bookish tastes; and besides he took every opportunity of inspiring them therewith. If he wished to entice them to Vaucluse by a picture of the delights of the place, it was always the library he mentioned first. He was proud to be able to put at their disposition every kind of book, the entire chorus of the Muses; and he held that these pleasures, along with walking and friendship, should be enough for the happiness of such lofty spirits as were those he loved. When in Lombardy, he begged Guido Sette, then at the papal court, to go as often as he could to Vaucluse. "The friend's house, the country bed, the garden, all are his. Only let him give a look to the plantation, and shake the dust from the books, in mourning for the absence of the master."

During the poet's stay in Provence he was sometimes called to Avignon on business, where he had to remain for some time. The library was not then closed to his intimates. One neighbour in particular, the Bishop of Cavaillon, Philip de Cabassoles, did not scruple to use it. Petrarch complained one day of having missed one of his visits: "How could you pass five days at my house without me? . . . I should be very angry with you, if you had not, in the most charming way, somewhat righted the wrong you did me by using my books and keeping company with them day and night. I am astonished," he said, "that your noble spirit, surrounded by all the sacred writers, the historians, the philosophers and the poets, should have given a thought to looking at my poor personal compositions. . . . My farmer tells me that you wished for some books, but would not take them away without my leave. I beg you, do what you like with me and my belongings."

Petrarch's farmer at Vaucluse must not be forgotten when one speaks of the books whose simple and devoted guardian he was. Listen to his master's words in the touching letter where he tells of the death of this model servant of the man of letters: "He was a man of the fields; but he had more intelligence and urbanity than a townsman. I believe the earth has produced none more faithful. His admirable devotion made up entirely for the badness and the perfidy of all my other servants. . . . I had likewise entirely confided to him my person, my possessions and all the books I have in France. Though there are books of every kind, and the little volumes are mixed up with the big, I never found anything missing, not even out of its place, when I came back after long absences, one of which lasted three years. This unlettered man was yet a real friend of letters, and guarded with a special vigilance the books he knew were dear to me. From long habit he had even got to know the names of the books of the ancients, and to pick out from

any there my own modest works. He beamed all over with joy every time I put a book into his hands; he pressed it with a sigh against his bosom. Sometimes he named the author in a low voice; and, wonderful to relate, in the mere contemplation of these works he believed he grew wiser and happier." To such a degree had Petrarch's tastes, even his innocent manias, passed to his servant.

In 1347, while the poet could still count on this faithful guardian, he decided to return for the fifth time to Italy. The journey was to be a long one; for, afire with the patriotic hopes which Rienzi's attempt had roused in him, he meant to go to its support. Unhappily, at Genoa he learned of both the massacre of the Colonna and the fall of the tribune; and instead of going to Rome, to be present, as he had dreamed, at the resurrection of the republic, he bent his steps towards Parma, to take possession of a canonry. His stay in Italy lengthened out, nevertheless, and was marked by some important acquisitions. At Genoa he tried to console himself for his political discomfiture by the help of a very fine Horace filled with notes. In his house at Parma he had already collected a little library. His Virgil, for instance, had never left him; and he wrote in it, according to his habit, the record of the losses, so many and so cruel, he sustained in his friendships. He had also his Abelard with him, to whom he confided, in the crises

of his conscience, the most intimate of all his
memories. In November, 1348, he began to keep
a little gardening register in the margins of a volume containing Apuleius and Palladius. In 1350,
he set out for Rome for the Jubilee, and went
through Florence and Tuscany, where his com-
patriots received him with affection for himself
and pride in his fame. There he reaped a full har-
vest of books. At Arezzo he discovered a Quinti-
lian, and on his return to northern Italy, passing
several days at Mantua, he bought Pliny's Natural History. Next year he left all his collection at
Verona, in charge of Guglielmo da Pastrengo, a
humanist worker like himself, with whom he had
formed a new and close friendship. He was ar-
ranging to go back to France, but with the intention of making only a short stay, and of returning promptly to settle in Italy. To Boccaccio, from
Verona, on June first, 1351, he wrote, "I intend
passing the end of summer in my quiet solitude
on the banks of the clear and rippling Sorgue,
amid the woods, the streams, and all those books
which, under the care of a rustic guardian, have
awaited me in silence more than four years. If
I took the road again to Italy before that, I fear
the excessive heat might overwhelm this poor
body, used nevertheless to fatigue from childhood, and which I only spare that I may reserve
for it still more arduous labours. But autumn, I
hope, may bring me, and along with me, my

books, which I have decided to join to my Italian library."

Hardly was Petrarch back in Vaucluse before he was bound again by the chain of the sweet old ways. He writes to his friends in Italy, "Let me look again at my leisure on the little gardens planted by my hands, and the woods so dear to my studies, and let me bring out my books from the bottom of their locked-up cupboard (clausi arculis et clavibus) to the light they have missed so long. Here, too, I have a good number, and they have their charm. I want to turn my eyes on them again, and have them turn their eyes on me. At least I fain would shake out the worms and the damp from the oldest parchments." Some volumes had, indeed, suffered from these book-scourges, which play havoc in shut-up houses, and which were Petrarch's terror. Many of the friends of his thought had grown old like those among the living, and he had more difficulty in recognizing them after so long a separation and a life so agitated and so diverse. "In entering my library once more I felt almost a stranger, not only among the ancients, but also before my own books. It needed a certain time and some effort to be once more on intimate terms." However, it was not long before he brought new guests in. He again began his searches at Avignon, and had the good fortune, in 1351, just when he was setting himself to his work on Roman history, to put his

hand on the Livy which long ago had served him
in his first studies.

In the autumn of 1352 he made his preparations
for departure. It was a serious removal he was
undertaking, and there was much weeding to be
done in his library. Petrarch left a few volumes,
some thirty or so; for he wished to be able to find
something to occupy himself with at Vaucluse
when he should return, as he meant to do now
and then. He selected also the papers he wished
to take with him. There was an enormous quan-
tity! Materials for books to be written, rough
drafts of Italian verses, to be arranged later on at
Padua, minutes of letters, a part of which found
place later in the first books of the Familiares,
correspondence of friends which he kept affec-
tionately, but of which he had to make up his
mind to lose some part with every change of residence. At last the house was in order; all was
ready, and the cavalcade took the road to Genoa.

The first day they were to cross the Durance
before sunset, and Petrarch stopped at Cavaillon
to receive the blessing of the good bishop. The
bishop was ill, and insisted on keeping him. Violent
torrents of rain had, however, begun to fall; the
streams were swollen; and the traveller, trem-
bling for his books, which the rain might spoil,
thought of leaving them in a safe place, and having them sent on later. He spent the night with
Philip de Cabassoles; but the news was brought

that the neighbourhood of Nice was infested by armed bands, which were cutting off all communications. Capricious as usual, he was delighted to find so many good reasons for retracing his steps. Besides, he would hardly have been able to travel without watching over his treasured boxes as he rode along. "I had with me," he says, "very precious baggage, my books, and along with them those modest writings with which I cover the papyrus of Memphis. I had no fear for myself, used as I am to bearing any hardships, but I own that I trembled for those beloved burdens. What was I to do? Was it not the will of God that I should not depart? I left several servants to continue the journey to Italy, and I returned to enjoy my solitude, all the profounder for their absence." It was six months more that Petrarch gave to Vaucluse. At last he left, little thinking that it was forever.

Italy kept her poet to herself for the one and twenty last years of his life. Save for two short journeys as ambassador, to the emperor Charles at Prague and to John the Good at Paris, he remained faithful to the country of his race and of his heart. But fêted, drawn hither and thither, invited by princes and by cities, a prey likewise to that restlessness of mind which threw him ceaselessly from noisy courts into silent retreats, and again from solitude back to active life, he never settled anywhere so long as he had dwelt on the banks of the Sorgue. When at last he thought he had found in his country home at Arquà something to make up for his beloved Helicon of Provence, he died before he had fully tasted its delights.

During the first years of his return he stayed principally at Milan, in a quiet house at the end of the town, very near the church of Saint Ambrose. As at Vaucluse, he rose at midnight. After the few hours of sleep which were all he needed, he went to his library, adjoining his bedroom, and every day dawn found him already long at work. A very severe winter, when the ink froze in the ink-pots, made no difference in his habits, and did his health no harm. He withstood the cold, thanks to the long woollen cloak which entirely enveloped him, and the benefits of which he wished to procure for his dear Boccaccio. His only illness came to him from a side where he least expected it. "I possess," he writes to a friend, "a big volume containing the letters of Cicero. To have it within my reach, I used to place it—you have seen me— at the entrance of my library, leaning against the jamb of the door. As I went in one day, thinking of something else as usual, I touched it accidentally with the edge of my gown. It fell and bruised my left leg just above the heel. Laughingly I cried out, 'What, friend Cicero, wouldst thou beat me?' Cicero held his tongue, but next day when I came in, he struck me again, and once more I

picked him up with a jest. In short, after I had been hurt several times, I lost my temper; and seeing he was displeased at being left on the ground, I put him on a shelf. But by this time the skin had been cut by the repeated blows, and a rather serious wound was the result." Petrarch, who suffered from bad circulation in his legs, was ill for nearly a year. One may guess the many jests that were passed about the trick which ungrateful Cicero had played on the most zealous of his servants. The studio to which this story introduces us must have been a somewhat narrow room, like those we see in the miniatures illustrating the homes of students of the time. One may imagine Petrarch seated on a wooden settle, his feet resting on a stool, in front of him a desk with an inkstand let into it. On the desk lay a great volume, with copper clasps, open so as to show the closely written columns. He is taking notes, pen in one hand, eraser in the other. By his side, on a lectern, is another open volume for reference. Along the wall, which is pierced by a single window, runs a shelf laden with books in manycoloured bindings. There are others on smaller shelves at the side of the writing-table. Every corner is utilized for books, and as a defence against the mice, a cat is curled up under his settle. Study bows the poet's head. Round him is that atmosphere of meditation best bred in little rooms where all the books are at hand.

The Library of Petrarch — Of the admirers of Petrarch who visited him at Milan, in his library, which was his usual reception-room, he loved to recall two, whose remembrance was particularly gratifying to his vanity, Pandolfo Malatesta and Niccolo Acciajuoli. Malatesta, who was ill, was carried in his servant's arms to the poet's house, to enjoy the pleasure of seeing him surrounded by books in his natural milieu. The other, who was grand seneschal of the kingdom of Sicily, had come to Milan to visit both Galeazzo Visconti and the old friend of king Robert. "Your Maecenas," he wrote to Zanobi da Strada, "did not disdain to come to see me in my library, in spite of the crowd by which he is surrounded all the time, of the business he had to do, and the length of the way to my house.... The great man came, with lowered fasces, as Pompey came long ago to Posidonius.... He crossed my humble threshold, uncovered before me, and almost bowed to the ground, as might an inhabitant of Parnassus entering the temple of Apollo and the Muses. His generous humility excited the respect of myself and the noble personages who were present, and all but moved us to tears. He showed much delicate interest in my collection of books, companions and nourishment of my repose, and even in each of them individually. Nothing could have been more agreeable, and we talked for long about a thousand things, and above all of you."

The year before Acciajuoli's visit he had re- ceived another, less flattering to his vanity, but dearer to his heart. Boccaccio had spent several days at Milan with him, and had even been present at the planting of some laurels in his garden. The traveller returned to Florence, with memory and heart full of his talks with the master; and his recollections of these formed the staple of conversation in the little circle where Petrarch was so passionately loved. A common friend, Francesco Nelli, in a letter to Petrarch, tells how he regretted he had not shared the delight, adding, "He tasted with his hands, his eyes, his ears, the magnificent collection of books, and what makes books precious,—their contents. For such favours of fortune he declares himself blest; and as for me, I hold him the happiest of men."

During Petrarch's sojourn at Milan, a change took place in the direction of his mind, and consequently in the contents of his library. To profane letters, which till then had solely occupied him, he added sacred literature. It was the Christian evolution of his conscience that led him to the decision of which he spoke to Nelli, a churchman ready to understand him: "I am going to speak to you of the new and already strong impulse that draws my pen and my mind towards holy books. Let the proud mock, who are repelled by the austerity of the words of God, as eyes accustomed to the gay apparel of courtesans are hurt

by the modest dress of some chaste mother of a
family. The Muses and Apollo, I believe, tolerate,
nay, even approve the design I have formed.
Having given up my youth to youthful studies,
I purpose to reserve my ripe age for more serious cares. ... But in giving preference to certain
authors, I do not reject the others. If Saint Jerome
claims to have done so, his own style belies him.
... As for language, if the subject require it, I
shall keep Cicero and Virgil as my models. For
the conduct of my life—though I have much to
learn from them—I shall rather follow the counsels of those guides whose teaching tends to sal-
vation without danger of error."

For a moment Petrarch was unfaithful to his
exclusive worship of Antiquity. He, the profane
poet, tried to walk in spiritual ways. From his first
steps therein he was able to satisfy his pious curiosity without difficulty, at Linterno, in the company of his country neighbours, the monks of
Garegnano, and at Milan, in the library of Saint
Ambrogio, of which he expressly speaks in one
of those half-philosophic, half-religious treatises,
which he took delight in composing. From this
time his collection of ecclesiastical writers increased. In 1355 he received from Florence a su-
perb manuscript of the kind,—Saint Augustine's
Commentary on the Psalms. Boccaccio sent it to
him; and it was a special treasure, first for the
author's sake, then for David, whose admirer he

proclaims himself to be, and lastly as a remembrance of a generous friend. But at the same time we are assured that his new interests had not entirely thrust aside his ancient studies by the fact that he was having the History of Augustus copied at Verona.

Petrarch added to his library in three different ways,—by gifts, by purchases, and by having copies made. All his friends worked to help him. Although in the retouching, done with a view to publication, many familiar details have vanished, his correspondence still contains a certain number of requests for books and thanks for those sent. More especially is this the case in his letters to Lapo da Castiglioncho; to Nelli, who seems to have been always on the lookout on his account; to Pastrengo, from whose library he might freely borrow; to Bruni, who sends him a packet from Avignon; to John of Parma, who gave him a fine map of the world on parchment; above all to Boccaccio, who procured for him the most various works,—a Dante, for instance, follows a Saint Augustine,—and who even presented him with copies of Varro and Cicero transcribed by his own hand, thereby adding a great charm to the books, says Petrarch. What zeal, what devotion, did they show in seconding the least of his desires! He had expressed a wish to read an ecclesiastical work of little importance, the Life of Peter Damian, and thought that it might possibly be found at Ravenna, the holy man's own city. Boccaccio passing there, set himself at once to search for it, first among the monks, and then among private persons, but all in vain. At last an old man took him to his house, and pointed out a stack of dusty, mildewed books. He rummaged among them with disgust, found nothing of interest, and was just going away discouraged when he caught sight of the wished-for title on a slender booklet all soiled and stained. He carried it away joyfully, and made haste to copy it and send it to Petrarch, though the style of the work seemed to him insipid and unworthy of the writer awaiting it.

Petrarch's friends were keen rivals in their desire to help him. The worthy Nelli found a means of being ever in his thoughts: he sent him a breviary for the recitation of the daily office. But the volume was of some value, and the poet refused to take it as a gift. We may guess the sense of his answer by the following note from the prior of the Holy Apostles: "I thought you were not to speak any more about that little present. If you force me to mention it again, beware: I shall be vexed. By the sweetness of your noble friendship, the dearest thing in all the world to me, I assure you that the book was really mine, and no one made use of it. I pretended it belonged to some one else, for I was afraid you would refuse it from delicacy, and I was sorry for the annoyance caused you by the inconvenient copy which you were

using. As for fixing the price of the volume, without any false shame, as you say, you could not
bid me do anything more ridiculous. No, you
speak to a deaf man. Elsewhere you may find
me a simpleton, but here I have my eyes open,
and refuse to be caught. Place some bounds to
your pride. Let a poor man who is devoted to you
offer you a little book. One must not always be
giving, but must learn to take as well. Is not the
former pleasure the sweeter? Let your friend enjoy it now and then. And no more of this business; all else you write is a joy, but this annoys
me." This note bears witness to the only dispute
that occurred in their friendship.

The poet's tastes were known throughout all
Italy. Humble persons tried to win his favour by
the gift of a volume. He himself explored the convents of northern Italy, the libraries of princes and
of private persons, making use of the respect by
which he was surrounded and his powerful con-
nections as keys to unlock all doors. He never he-
sitated to write to people he did not know, as soon
as he learned that they possessed books. "The ru-
mour runs that Cicero lodges under your roof and
that you have many and rare works of his genius.
Oh, happiness a hundred times greater than that of
Evander's who received Alcides! If you deem me
worthy, permit me to bask in the presence of such
a guest." The grammarian who was honoured by
this letter made haste to reply by sending all he

possessed of Cicero. Petrarch found nothing of importance save a rather good copy of the Tuculanes; nevertheless he returned thanks with perfect grace, and as if he had derived the utmost profit from the communication. When a book pleased him he did not hesitate to make a considerable outlay to obtain it. To Nelli he wrote, in 1362, regarding purchases which were doubtless of importance: "Do not put off; keep your promise. Get me this new addition to the library which is all the repose and all the relaxation of my mind, the whole joy of my existence. By all the saints, make haste, and trust in the resources of my little purse. When you send it to me I shall think myself the happiest of men, and already with the mere hope of it my spirits rise. Nevertheless, if I must be content with the books I have, since they are fairly numerous and of some value, I shall still count myself richer than Croesus, and shall look on the treasures of our rich people as of very little value." He was not always lucky in his negotiations. He speaks often and with vehemence of those bibliophiles for show, who keep useful books "prisoners," who "beg them, and track them, and snatch them" from workers. Probably he had a grievance against some more fortunate rival. He took his revenge in attributing to books a silent indignation "at belonging so often to idle, selfish men, when so many scholars were craving them." Far from diminishing with

age, Petrarch's passion seemed to increase, till it became more and more like the foible of a collector. He acknowledged it with a good grace. "In my business letters books are always the chief subject. I own I am greedy for them. This love has consumed me ever since my youth. Some will say it is folly. What is more foolish than to seek what you cannot use when you have got it? Horace laughed at the weakness: 'Siquis emat citharas'—you know the rest. But no one who knows anything of the letters of Cicero will be much surprised at my taste. That great spirit, who, like a fountain clear and inexhaustible, poured out the works that do most honour to the ancient Latin world, reveals himself in his letters as not merely anxious for, but passionately desirous of the works of others." To Giovanni d'Incisa he made the same confession, pleading his cause in another way: "Do not think of me as sheltered from the ills of mankind. There is within me an unquenchable desire which I have never been able to suppress, nor have I desired to suppress it; for I flatter myself that the desire for worthy things can never be unworthy. Would you know my complaint? I cannot satisfy my hunger for books (libris satiari nequeo), even when I have already more perhaps than are needful to me. But this search is like others: success only sharpens the edge of desire. Moreover, books have a charm which is theirs alone: gold and silver, pearls and purple raiment, mansions of marble, well-tilled fields, horses with fine trappings, all these and their like – afford but a dumb and shallow pleasure. Books alone give delight to the very marrow of one's soul; they speak to us; they counsel us; they become an intimate and living part of us" (Libri medullitus delectant, colloquuntur, consulunt nobis, et viva quadam nobis atque arguta familiaritate junguntur). Petrarch is here truly inspired by his subject. Never has a more noble passion had a more eloquent defence.

His book-hunting extended very far. "When my friends left me," he says, "and when, according to their wont, they asked me if I desired anything from their country, I answered that I wanted nothing but books, and above all Cicero's books; I gave them notes concerning these, emphasizing the matter in conversation and in writing. Ah, the prayers I have addressed, the money I have sent, not only to Italy, but to France, to Germany, even to Spain and England – nay, would you believe it? – to Greece!" One such request remains written to a friend: "If you love me, commission some trustworthy and educated persons to wander about Tuscany to forage among the bookshelves of monks and other friends of study, and endeavour to find something which will appease – though it may irritate – my thirst. Although you know well enough in what waters I am used to fish, and in what woods I like to hunt,

yet that you may not go wrong, I enclose in my letter the list of what I particularly desire. That you may be the more zealous I tell you that I have sent the same requests to other friends in England, France and Spain. Do not let me think that any of those have surpassed you in devotion and in shrewdness."

Petrarch did not exaggerate the extent of the field of his investigations. In England he was for some time in relations with Richard de Bury; in northern France he had friends on whom he might count for more than one literary service; at Liège the archdeacon Matthew Longus was his correspondent; in Germany he had Sacramor de Pommiero and Jean Ocko, the bishop of Olmütz. Even from the East, an envoy of the emperor Nicholas Sygeros, who had known him at Avignon, sent him a text of Homer. To thank him Petrarch wrote one of the happiest of his letters, and begged from him Hesiod and Euripides, that he might at least have the pleasure of seeing them in their Greek costume. Later, Leon Pilatus, when he left him to seek his fortune in Constantinople, promised to bring him back some Greek authors; and when Philip de Mézières, chancellor of Pierre de Lusignan, embarked for Cyprus, perhaps he, too, had received from the poet at Venice some warmly recommended list.

True, the greater part of his desiderata could not be satisfied. Without giving up hope, he consoled himself like a philosopher for so many repeated checks. "I am not surprised," he writes to one of his most zealous correspondents, "that you cannot lay your hands on the books I asked for. When I charged you to seek for them, I tried for success without much counting on it. Though often disappointed I cannot stop my search. It is good to hope for what one desires. I shall get the books that are possible to be got; but never shall ignoble discouragement hold me back from my splendid pursuit. Patiently I shall keep within me the desire for what I lack, content with what fate has already given me, calming my passion for reading and knowledge by meditation on death." He got pleasure, too, from volumes of which he already had duplicates. The arrival of a more correct or better written text was enough to rejoice his heart; he devoured it; could not take his eyes off it till, like the thirsty leech, he had drunk his fill. He could not even eat or sleep. One evening at Monza a monk brought him a volume just before he sat down to table. The poet opened it, forgot his meal, and did not return to ordinary life till he had read the whole.

One can imagine with what transports he received the books left behind at Vaucluse, when they reached Milan after escaping a great peril. Thieves had broken into the house on the Sorgue and had pillaged it. The books, which had been stolen with the rest of the things, were found —

how, it is not known—thrown into a ditch as useless booty, or sold to a pawnbroker at Avignon. Devoted friends sent them back to the poet, who deemed himself lucky to have saved from the disaster the possession he valued most. Petrarch was the complete book-lover. He attached value to the accessories of a book, to material, ornamentation, and binding. Not one of the manuscripts of his collection which have been found is on paper. Old or new, they are all on parchment. The greater part of those which were certainly executed for him are on fine vellum, prepared with care and chosen by a connoisseur. He apologized for offering a book which was not fresh and had grown yellow. His own were often elegantly, sometimes richly, decorated. We know the large miniature he asked of Simone Martini, to place at the head of his Virgil. Four other volumes contain an important series of miniatures, two at least of which are contemporary; and this proves, far more than does the Virgil, .. serious interest in the art

Che alluminare è chiamata in Parisi.

He paid due attention also to binding, for the safeguard it assured to the written thought. It is the last of the operations—of which he is pleased to give the list—which are necessary to definitely constitute a book. But there is nothing to indicate that the binding was done in his own house, as it was in Richard de Bury's. For certain works, and for some presents, he permitted a rich binding; and in presenting a volume to Pandolfo Malatesta, he regretted not having been able to superintend the final operations. "If I had been on the spot," he says, "I should have had a silk cover made, and, at least, silver clasps." Doubtless, his own favourite books were bound in that fashion.

One may hazard a guess at Petrarch's palaeological tastes. He had no respect for the fashionable caligraphy of the time, arranged in fine columns, "the effect of which is attractive at a distance, but looked at near wants clearness and distracts the eye." In the books which he had transcribed, he demanded clearness before anything else; and what he praised most in one of his copyists was his clear and careful writing, which easily caught the eye. As for ancient manuscripts, his predilections are revealed to us in a letter of thanks to Boccaccio, who had sent him a magnificent Saint Augustine. He admired the book specially for its ample size, the sobriety of its ornament, and the majesty of the antique type (vetustioris litterae majestas). And he was particularly pleased with the fine small characters of the tenth and eleventh centuries, which still fascinate palaeographists to-day. The taste which reigned in Italy in the fifteenth century for the lettera antica, had Petrarch for its pioneer; and

76

he strove against the angular, heavy, massive character of the trecento script. Even his own handwriting was transformed by the influence of his reading: the habit which his eyes had contracted gave it that clear and elegant personal character we know in his autographs, which was much admired by his contemporaries.

Above everything else Petrarch sought good texts. Whether he had them copied at home or elsewhere, accuracy was his chief care. When he was lucky enough to find correct grammar and spelling, he appreciated them; but above all he laid stress on respect for the author's sense, with which the copyists about him took such liberties. He complained especially that there was no regular apprenticeship to guarantee their work. "Admitting that the texts are perfect, what remedy is there for the ignorance and carelessness of copyists, who confuse and corrupt everything? This fear, I believe, has dissuaded many eminent men from writing great works. Just punishment for an indolent age, zealous in the kitchen and indifferent to literature, which tests the skill of cooks, and not of scribes! Whoso can scratch a parchment and drive a quill, passes for a copyist, however lacking he may be in knowledge, intelligence, and craftsmanship. I do not ask spelling from them, which has long since disappeared; but would to God they could reproduce, no matter how, what they are given to copy! Their insufficiency would still be evident; but at least the substance of the text would not disappear. Instead of this, our scribes confuse the original with the copy; set out to write one thing and write something else, so that an author can no longer recognize his own words. If Livy or Cicero, or any of the ancients, but above all if Pliny, returned to earth, and reread their own works, would they know them again? Would they not be continually at a loss, and think they were reading, here the work of another man, and there that of a barbarian?... The noblest achievements of man are perishing; in great part have already perished. Our age, insensible to the evil, offers no remedy. The loss of literature is accounted as nothing; some even regard it as a benefit. And now to add to this disdain, to this hatred of the finest thing on earth, comes the havoc played by copyists subject neither to rule nor test. Such license is not granted to blacksmiths, nor to labourers, nor to weavers, nor in any of the other crafts, where, nevertheless, the harm done would be less. This professional one is open to all; every one rushes to it, certain of drawing pay for spoiling everything."

He had adopted the plan of having some young men in his house, whom he trained as copyists. Such assistance became more and more necessary to him as his works increased in number; for he was obliged to send copies to the great per-

sonages of his acquaintance, who used to ask for them, as well as to his ever eager friends. He liked also to circulate the little known books in his library amongst those whom he knew would appreciate them. And he delighted to make known such as had brought moral support to himself—Saint Augustine, for instance, which he gave to his brother, to Donato degli Albanzani, and to others as well, hoping they would derive from it a like benefit. In order to satisfy all his needs, he kept by him during his last years a certain number of copyists. "I am accustomed," he said, in describing his mode of life, "to have five or six by me; for the time being, there are only three, because one can find no real copyists, but only scribes (pictores), and even these have no talent." Boccaccio in one of his letters refers to the young men his friend had about him. They accompanied Petrarch on his travels; and he had the satisfaction of seeing their work grow under his eyes. He himself has noted the various stages in the execution of a manuscript still in existence: Domi scriptus, Patavi ceptus, Ticini perfectus, Mediolani illuminatus, et ligatus anno 1369. Giovanni Malpaghini of Ravenna, the copyist of this book, a translation of the Iliad, has left a name in literary history. Petrarch, with whom he lived for many years, educated him and treated him as a son. He was a man of admirable gifts, and capable of rendering great services. As secretary he

The Library of Petrarch was employed in the most delicate affairs, entrusted with the care of keeping the poet's papers in order, and of classifying such letters as Petrarch wished to preserve. The task was difficult, and several of the master's friends who had attempted it had been obliged to give it up. He accomplished it single-handed, and helped to form the collection of the Familiares which later he transcribed. Not so complicated, but of a no less intimate character was his task of making the final copy of the Canzoniere, which the poet himself finished. He stopped halfway in copying the translation of Homer made by Pilatus at Florence; for at that time, weary of the life he led in Petrarch's house, and of his honourable slavery in the service of an exacting old man, Malpaghini asked for his liberty, and left suddenly. A painful scene took place between him and the master, which Petrarch described at length in a letter to Donato degli Albanzani. The one fact that is clear in the dispute is that the profession of a copyist had ended by disgusting the young secretary. "I do not wish to copy any more," he declared. Although Petrarch denied it, he had evidently abused both his scribe's pen and his zeal. He was punished for it, and never got over the loss of so intelligent a companion and so valuable a collaborator.

Petrarch had by that time left the states of the Visconti. From 1362 to 1368 he lived chiefly at

Venice, and he even drew thither his son-in-law and daughter. As soon as he had settled he sent for all the books which he had left in other towns. "If the volume is completed, as I think," he wrote to Modio of Parma, "have it illuminated and handsomely bound by master Benedetto, and send me the copy and the original in the baggage of Gioannolo of Como. Messer Danisolo will pay whatever is due, and my Francescuolo, who knows these friends very well, will give you any advice you may need in the matter. Think rather of my trust in you than my importunity." And so the collection was transported to the lagoons. While at Venice, Petrarch narrates that he received a visit in his library from an Averroist, who came to ridicule Saint Augustine, and that he was obliged to show him the door. He also describes in vivid dramatic style the reception of the Latin translation of Homer, which "delighted all the Greek and Latin inmates of the library." Boccaccio, in his turn, arriving in Venice in his friend's absence, and welcomed by his daughter Francesca, wrote to him that dear "Tullia" had placed the books at his disposal during his stay there.

In the month of May, 1362, while at Padua, the poet received a curious letter from Boccaccio. The writer of the Corbaccio had been converted: for him there was to be no more poetry, no more profane reading. He was going to give up his studies,

**The Library of Petrarch** sell his books, and burn whatever Italian works he possessed, many of which were coarse and immoral. A Carthusian of Siena had found him out, endoctrinated, and converted him. His fiery sermons had disturbed the easy-going and charming nature. Petrarch answered him in a noble dissertation full of a truly Christian philosophy, in which he did his best to appease the scruples of Boccaccio. Could not he change his conduct, and respond to the appeal of grace, without breaking with all that was best in his past, and renouncing the work which had strengthened his mind? Moreover, if he really meant to carry out his project, here is his old friend's suggestion to him: "If you absolutely wish to get rid of your books, I like to think that you would prefer me to any other purchaser. You are right in speaking of my greed for books, and if I denied it, my writings would belie me. It seems to me that on this occasion I should only be buying what ought to fall to me. On the other hand, I do not want the library of a man such as you to be scattered, and to pass into profane hands. Although separated in body, we have lived together in spirit; so I desire that our collection may remain united after us. If God assents to my wish, it shall go intact to a pious and saintly abode, where we shall always be kept in remembrance (haec supellex nostra post nos ... ad aliquem nostri perpetuo memorem, pium ac devotum locum, simul inde ex-

cerpta perveniat). As to naming a price for the purchase of your books, as you kindly propose, I cannot do it, not knowing exactly either their titles, their number, or their value. Make an accurate note of these in a letter. Thus, if ever you decide to do what I have always desired and which you once promised me, namely, to come and spend together the poor remainder of our lives, you will see your books again in my home among those which I have collected, and which are yours also; and you will then perceive that, far from losing anything, it will rather have been a gain to you." Owing to the remonstrances of Petrarch, Boccaccio softened the exaggeration of his penitence. But his friend was still looking out for a means of avoiding the dispersal of his own library. He decided to offer it to the Republic of Venice, or rather to the church of Saint Mark, under whose shadow, doubtless, he now desired to end his life in peace.

In that same year, 1362, he had experienced, to his own cost, the want of security in northern Italy. Having left Padua to go to France, where the pope summoned him and Vaucluse drew him, he was obliged to retrace his steps because Piedmont was ravaged by war. He then turned towards Germany in response to the emperor's invitation to visit him; but this also he had to give up, for the road was no safer. Such annoyances were the more distressing, hampered as he was

by his library, from which he could no longer
separate himself. After many tremblings for this
precious treasure, he had taken refuge in Venice
"with his books and his pens," happy to find pro-
tection "in this haven open to all mankind." The
position of the town sheltered it from continen-
tal warfare; and already it exercised that charm
which leads scholars to believe that nowhere else
in all the world could they work so well. Finally,
the friendship of many cultivated men, and especially that of the devoted Benintendi, chancellor of the Republic, held the poet there. Petrarch
decided to settle definitely in Venice. Obliged,
however, to keep up a fairly large household,
and uncertain, in the troubled state of Italy, of
receiving his income regularly, he was forced to
think of assuring his material position. If Saint
Mark would house him, he might, in return, leave
the church his books, the dispersal of which he
dreaded. Benintendi, who had been consulted on
this subject, offered to arrange the business. Petrarch saw the project growing in his mind. But
already he dreamed of nothing less than the
foundation of a great public library which the
Venetian state was to take over after his death,
and from which posterity would derive such services as had aforetimes been rendered by the
great collections of antiquity whose history he
had read. "If we succeed," he wrote to the chancellor, "it will certainly be, I dare not say a glory,

but assuredly the path to glory, for you, your descendants and the Republic. Many things that have become great and famous have sprung from as humble beginnings." And he imagined the spirit of their friend the doge, Andrea Dandolo, rejoicing in Paradise over this project, in no way jealous of having left to one of his successors "the honour of founding a public library." The poet insisted, moreover, on not considering himself as the person most benefited in this matter: it was a service which he wished to render the state far more than an advantage which he asked for himself. "Weary no one with importunate requests," he told the chancellor; "do whatever is necessary and in accordance with our discretion. If the love of public welfare did not impel us to take the initiative, it is we who should be entreated." Benintendi brought a proposition before the senate, in the poet's name and written in his own hand in chancery Latin, which shows ingenuously enough, and very clearly, the double passion of his life, his love of books and of fame: "Francesco Petrarca desires, if it be the will of Christ and of the blessed Mark the Evangelist, to make the church of Saint Mark heir to a certain number of books which he now has, or which he may one day possess, on condition that they shall not be sold or scattered in any way whatsoever, but shall be preserved forever in a specially selected place, well protected from fire and water, in honour of the memory of the donor, and also for the consolation and benefit of the scholars and nobles of this town who are able to enjoy them. In desiring this, he does not claim that the books are either very numerous or very precious, but he cherishes the hope that later on this glorious city may, from time to time, add others at the expense of the state, and that private persons of noble mind, who love their country, and even strangers, following the example given, may bequeath, by their last testament, some part of their possessions to the said church; and that thus the collection will become a great and famous library equal to those of antiquity. What glory this state will derive therefrom, the wise and the ignorant must alike understand. If this comes to pass, by the help of God and the illustrious patron of your city, Francis will rejoice and call himself happy in the Lord for having, in some way, been the source of so great a benefit. He may perhaps write again, at greater length, on this subject if the matter is followed up. . . . In the meantime, for himself and the said books, he would wish to have not a large but a suitable house, in order that no unfortunate circumstance may prevent the realization of his plan; and he himself would gladly reside in the city, provided that he can do so with comfort. He cannot be absolutely sure on account of numerous difficulties. None the less he hopes this."

A contract was drawn up between the poet and the Republic, the existence of which is attested by its solemn acceptance registered by the Grand Council. On the fourth of September, 1362, this assembly adopted the following resolution: "Considering how the glory of God and that of the blessed Mark the Evangelist, and the honour and fame of this our city, will be served by the proposal of Messer Francis Petrarch (whose glory is such throughout the whole world that there has not been, in the memory of man, and there is not now in Christendom, any moral philosopher or poet whose fame can be compared to it), his offer will be accepted according to the terms of the note written in his hand. Henceforth the Monte shall charge itself with the expense of his house and dwelling for the duration of his life." The house placed at the poet's disposal was the Palazzo delle due Torri on the Riva dei Schiavoni.

It was not Petrarch's fault, one sees, that the Bibliotheca Marciana was not founded a century earlier. At a time when all libraries, even the papal one, were of a strictly private character, he had the first idea of a public foundation, to which all workers should be freely admitted. This generous plan for the furtherance of literature was to be taken up again, in the same city of Venice, by Cardinal Bessarion, and it is very improbable that Petrarch's idea was unknown to the distinguished churchman. Furthermore, if the first projects, welcomed with such eagerness by the Signoria, were not put into execution at Petrarch's death, it was not, as has often been said, due to the carelessness of the Venetians, but for more powerful reasons which no one could have foreseen at the time of the donation.

Here, summed up in a few words, is what my researches have been able to discover regarding the somewhat obscure history of the dispersal of the famous library. At the time of Petrarch's death his books were on Paduan territory, and Francis of Carrara, the lord of Padua, was on bad terms with the Venetian Republic. He seems to have thrown obstacles in the way of delivering the library, which he authorized the heirs to sell, and of which he reserved for himself the lion's share. Although several of Petrarch's manuscripts may be found scattered in various Italian hands in the fifteenth century, most of them remained for a time with Carrara's at Padua. If Venice asserted her claim, the great war known as that of Chioggia, in which the Republic was on the point of perishing, definitely settled the question. But the victor did not keep his literary treasures long. Too eager to imitate the exploits of the Roman hero, whose likeness he had had painted in his palace by the advice of Petrarch, Francis of Carrara kindled the war against Venice, and was at last crushed by the alliance of the Venetian state with that of Gian Galeazzo Visconti. All his pos-

sessions fell to the lord of Milan, and it was this prince, an equally great friend of letters, who collected Petrarch's books in the library of the castle at Pavia. A century later, again by right of war, they passed into the hands of Louis XII, king of France. After his conquest of the Milanese, in 1499, they were transferred to the castle of Blois. And so it came about that, after so many changes, most of the books which belonged to Petrarch are to be found to-day in the Bibliothèque Nationale at Paris, the heir to the literary possessions of the French kings. Twenty-seven volumes are there; seven others in the Vatican; one (the Virgil) is in the Ambrosian Library at Milan; another (the Horace) is in the Laurentian at Florence; one is in the Marcian Library at Venice; one is at Padua, and one at Troyes in Champagne. So far I have not been able to trace the others.*

In his offers to the Republic, the poet had formally reserved to himself complete freedom of residence, including the right of carrying with him his library, from which he was never separated. After a several years' stay in Venice, broken by many journeys, he grew tired of a city where he met too many Averroist philosophers, and where he missed the garden which had come

*The description of all these volumes and the abstract of Petrarch's curious marginal notes may be found in my Petrarque et l'Humanisme.

to be a necessity. Little by little he lengthened his stays at Padua, where he was happy in performing his duties as a canon, and in the friendship of Francis da Carrara, a truly cultivated prince. Finally, pressed by Carrara, and the requirements of his health, for which mountain air was necessary, Petrarch decided to leave the lagoons and to divide his time between Padua and the village of Arquà, in the Euganean hills, where the lord of Padua had given him a country estate. Besides, the nearness of Venice allowed him to return there easily and to keep up his friendships in that city. In the beginning of 1368, his books were still there, entrusted to the care of Messer Donato degli Albanzani; but they soon rejoined their master. To increase his property at Arquà, Petrarch had, in 1370, purchased a piece of land with his own money, and thus signified his intention of living in the domains of Carrara.

In this mountain hermitage, surrounded by the peaceful landscape on which the house he built still looks down, Petrarch lived again in his old age the years at Vaucluse. "I still maintain," he wrote, "the modest mode of life of my earlier days, which I consider the most profitable and the pleasantest. I have grown richer only in years, and in some books. . . . A great part of the time I remain in the country, desirous as ever of solitude and repose. To read, to write and to meditate are still, as in my youth, my life and

my delight. My only wonder is that after having applied myself to such arduous study, I have learned so little."

His scholarship, none the less, was as famous as his poetic genius. Constant appeals came both to his memory and to his books, which he generously placed at every one's disposal. Many were the visits and the requests he received; and he always kept in "his little cabinet" some good work to lend to a lover of letters. A gentleman of Ferrara wrote from Padua to Ludovico di Gonzaga, regarding a letter of Caesar's which he intended for him: "I believe that if any other work of that emperor has been preserved in the world, it belongs to our illustrious common lord, Messer Francesco Petrarca. The coffer and the shrine of the monuments of antiquity are with him, and no one can hope to discover anything which is not already in his possession. In a few days I shall go and visit him at Arquà, where he now is, and I shall press him to tell me which of Caesar's works he has. I need fear no refusal; always obliging to everybody, he has been especially so to me." The treasures gathered in the studios of Arquà and of Padua were considered by the master as a trust of which he owed an account to the students of his age, and never has book-lover been more generous with his riches, or more thoroughly convinced of the rights which study held over his collections.

At this time the tastes of his youth had once more asserted all their power. In his readings, sacred writers left a great place free for profane authors. In order to confide to them new observations, he took up again the books that had grown old with him, and were all the dearer. "Mecum seruit," he said of the Confessions of Saint Augustine. He had the joy of acquiring others, and at seventy he read them with the same enthusiasm which he would have felt at thirty. One of his last works was the great commentary he began on the margins of his Homer, but which he was never able to complete. In the peace of the country and of family life, surrounded by his daughter, his son-in-law, and a few friends, with a mind ripened by the experience of a long life, he questioned anew the works which had revealed to him the wisdom of antiquity. To all other knowledge he remained indifferent. Certain books on canon and civil law, which one of the Colonna had left with him, ran the risk, he thought, of going astray at his death. He desired earnestly to restore them to their owner, but he added frankly: "If they were the works of Cicero or Varro I should, perhaps, not be so pressing."

The last years of his life were far from peaceful. The war, which had long been smouldering between the lord of Padua and the Venetians, broke out at last, and residence outside city walls was no longer safe. Petrarch remained at Arquà

as long as possible, but although a friend declared that it would be sufficient for him to write his revered name over the door in order to turn aside the soldiers, he thought it more prudent to return to Padua. "To-day or to-morrow," he wrote on the seventeenth of November, 1373, "I expect my little family, who have remained in the country. As for the books I had there, I have brought them back, leaving the house and the rest in the care of God." This forced residence in Padua, which the war prolonged, was no loss to his work. His son-in-law, Francesco da Brossano, and especially his friend and disciple, Lombardo della Seta, who also lived with him and served him as his last secretary, took charge of his household and of his library. Material cares were thus spared him, and he found the necessary means for his researches garnered and at hand in the books which he had carefully annotated during his life and which were familiar to the people around him. But he grieved at not returning to the fields, and impatiently repeated the wish of Horace. He had to wait until the month of October, 1373, and after the defeat of Francesco of Carrara, had even to go to Venice with his friend's son, who went there to make honourable amends to the Signoria and to treat for terms of peace. It was only after this fatiguing mission that the aged poet, whose health was fast failing, could return to Arquà and enjoy once

The Library of Petrarch

more some months of study and meditation. On a July night in 1374, when Petrarch was keeping vigil in his small study, as was his wont, death came on him. His friends found him in the morning with his forehead resting on the book that lay open before him. Thus great Petrarch died, in fashion worthy of the love he felt for books and knowledge, which, far more than the lovely Provençal lady, had been the burning passion of his life.

# III
# PETRARCH AND HIS MASTERS
## VIRGIL AND CICERO

# III
## PETRARCH AND HIS MASTERS
## VIRGIL AND CICERO

### ಎ

### VIRGIL

### * *
### *

VIRGIL AND CICERO were the
great masters of Petrarch's mind:
"Questi son gli occhi della lingua
nostra." Many passages in his Latin works serve as commentaries
to this line in the Trionfo della
Fama. "I have loved Cicero and Virgil so well," he
once wrote, "that I could have loved none better.
Many of the great writers of antiquity have been
dear to me; but for these two dearer, I felt a filial
affection towards the one, and brotherly love for
the other. It was admiration as well as long famil-
iarity, bred by the study of these two men of genius, which kindled in me this feeling. My friendship could hardly have been as great for living
men I have seen." These friends of his became
the models for his pen. He studied them together
to form his Latin style on them; and even his
prose is as frequently tinged with reminiscences
of the Roman poet as of the orator. They were
the fathers of the language for him. The parallel

he drew between them from this point of view seems to have been one of his favourite ideas: "Our Cicero is the supreme father of Latin speech; Virgil comes just after him, or since disputes arise sometimes about their rank, let us call them both the fathers of Roman eloquence. . . . They have divided this splendid realm between them in such fashion that each remains within his boundaries without encroaching on the fame of the other." These two writers may be selected as typical examples of Petrarch's classical culture; and we can plainly trace the way in which he studied and understood them. Cicero early became his mind's chief guide. Virgil appealed specially to his heart, and developed his poetic gifts. In a single sentence he marked his predilection for the poet of manly tenderness. "To many Latin poets is praise due; to him alone admiration" (Cum multi vatum e numero nostrorum laudabiles, unus ille mirabilis est).

What did he know of Virgil's life? He had noted such hints as the poet permits to escape him in his verse; and knew, in fact, almost everything we ourselves have learned from ancient sources. He had even read the life of Virgil attributed to Donatus, and had used for biographical purposes the commentary of Servius. Indeed, it was from Servius he borrowed the legend of Cicero's friendship with the young Virgil, and he fills a letter with it. The tale was well calcu-

lated to please him. He was delighted to find a historical link between his favourite authors, and to think that they had known each other. In short, he had at least as much information as the first of Virgil's Renaissance biographers, Secco Polentone, who lived in the beginning of the following century. At Mantua he had searched for reminiscences of the master. Like many another after him he had wandered about the country round Pietola, where the poet was born; and had even addressed a charming epistle to Virgil, which, in spite of some imperfections of its poetic style, is imbued with the grace of the Bucolics. "I am writing these verses to you in the sweet quiet of your own fields. I tread the rough paths across the meadows, where you were wont to walk. Ever before my eyes are the banks of your stream, the inlets of your lake, the shadows of your woods, the slopes of your little hill, the grassy mound beside the pleasant fountain where you used to sit. And all these sights bring you near to me." In the neighbourhood of Naples he had enjoyed visiting the places described in the Aeneid, and had collected Virgilian legends, but with discretion and not with the foolish credulity of his time. "Fame, in the case of great men, is not satisfied with the praises of truth; it often opens the way for fables, too." In spite of his enlightenment, Boccaccio still believed, not only in the universal knowledge of Virgil, but also in his prodigies as an astrologer,—

in the bronze horse he had made which cured sick horses, and in a score of other tales equally ludicrous. Petrarch was free from all this credulity. In the very court of Avignon he had himself been suspected of magic just for his constant reading of Virgil: "It is really enough to make one laugh. I, who am more hostile than any one to soothsayers and magic, am accused of the black art because of my friendship for Virgil. Is this all I have studied for?" He revenged himself by covering with ridicule the priest who had dared to accuse him; and he determined to put an end to the absurd reputation with which popular credulity had for centuries invested the memory of his beloved poet. When he went on his journey to Naples, he found many memories of Virgil in the city and in the neighbourhood, all travestied by the popular imagination. Not a single jot of the legend of Virgil the magician would he accept. This question was then still discussed by cultivated people. Petrarch describes a conversation which he had with king Robert on the subject, while they were going through the tunnel of Piedigrotta, the piercing of which was commonly attributed to the poet's magic. "In the presence of many people, the king asked me what were my views on this subject. I answered jestingly that I had read no text which proved Virgil to be a magician. The king gravely agreed with me, and confessed that there was not the slightest trace

of magic on the rock, while there were marks of the boring tools which had been used." Not content with substituting a natural explanation for the tradition, Petrarch, after picturesquely describing the landscape, attempts an interpretation of the legend: "At the end of the dark passage, just where one begins to see the sky again, Virgil's own tomb can be seen on a height; it is a very ancient monument, and it may have given rise to the idea that the mountain had been tunnelled by the poet." Petrarch can easily be excused for having put faith in the authenticity of the "tomb of Virgil," which so many poets and travellers have celebrated since. In these matters it was chiefly the opinion of the vulgar fool (vulgus insulsum) which Petrarch had to combat. There was more real boldness of spirit in refuting the universal belief in a Virgil, the prophet of Christ, and in giving to the Fourth Eclogue a meaning different from the traditional interpretation. This question had frequently been discussed, of course, and Dante's allusions to it had caused his commentators, in the fourteenth century, to take it up afresh; but among mediaeval scholars there was, perhaps, not a single reader of Virgil who would have made such precise reservations on this subject as we find in the treatise on the Repose of Monks. "There is a text of the Bucolics and a text of the Aeneid which speaks of the empire of Augustus. . . . Although it is merely Caesar

who is referred to, a pious and devout reader
might think it was the emperor of the heavens,
whose advent on earth had been announced by
universal prophecies. The poet, who knew of
these, did not attempt to soar as high; he thought
of the coming of a Roman emperor, unable to
conceive of anything greater. If the true light
had shown before his eyes, he would, doubtless,
have turned his thoughts towards another event."
This passage is extremely precise, and it would
be unjust if we accused Petrarch here of timi-
dity; he unmistakably denies Virgil's gift of prophecy, and his merit in expressing so clear an
opinion was all the greater because, though he
had Saint Jerome on his side, he had against him
an authority which he always held so high—that
of Saint Augustine, who had been the first to see
in Virgil the herald of Christ.

The standpoint from which Petrarch appreciated Virgil was thus entirely different from that
of the scholars who had preceded him. And yet
he did not read him in the way we do; as we
shall see by examining the following passage in
which, I think, his reasons for admiring the writer of the Aeneid are sufficiently well summed
up: "If I am to speak out all my mind, there is
no Latin genius whom I would rank above Virgil. If he is understood, as I understand him,
every true admirer of his works will find a light
in each word hidden beneath the poetic cloud.

He will recognize serious truths in thoughts con- cealed in god-like language, and must confess that, though others may surpass him in learning, no one, perhaps, overtowers his genius. Can I say more than Macrobius, who, speaking of the four kinds of eloquence, did not hesitate to attribute all four to Virgil alone? His astonishing eloquence and, in Seneca's words, the truly godlike quality of his genius were lacking to him in prose; but I think no one who has ever once drunk at the Castalian spring can be ignorant of what he was able to do in poetry." Let us put aside the four kinds of eloquence united in Virgil; let us remember only that "in every word there was a light hidden beneath the poetic cloud." It is enough to show that Petrarch sought in Virgil, together with what we still discover, a something which we have ceased to find.

Petrarch's views on the nature of poetry are well known. In theory, poetry and allegory seemed to him inseparable; and the mission of the "poeta," the true poet, who made use of the noble Latin tongue, was to veil the truth under beautiful symbols. The vulgar were not to be allowed to gaze thereon. Thus would it become the more precious for those who had the knowledge and the patience to discover it. He reverted at various times to these ideas, and showed how he would apply them in his Latin works and especially in his Eclogues. Although he believed he included in his conception of poetry several ancient poets, it was chiefly regarding Virgil that he clearly defined his attitude. In the Bucolics he saw a continual allegory hidden even in the most trifling words. As for the Aeneid, there is no reason to be surprised that the De continentia Vergilii of Fulgentius should have directly inspired his interpretation. Although Petrarch does not actually mention this singular work, which had weighed so much on the reading of Virgil in the Middle Ages, it is unlikely that he had not read it. At least he accepted its fundamental idea which turned the whole of Aeneas' adventures into a vast allegory of human life. Here he shows himself no more advanced than Dante in his famous letter to Can Grande. His personal criticism, at times so independent, was crushed by the consensus of opinion (poetantium communis habet opinio); the only liberties he took were the free interpretation of the Virgilian allegory, and offering in matters of detail the explanations which best satisfied his reason or were most pleasing to his fancy.

When Petrarch was still a youth, hearing one day a "monster of envy" attack Virgil, he wrote some indignant verses to teach this Zoïlus that great abstract truths were concealed under poetic fictions. But it is not in this epistle, however curious it may be, that one should look for the entire idea of Petrarch. We find it, ripened and developed, in a letter of his old age which has

every likelihood of containing the exact sum-
mary of his moral reflection on Virgil. Having
been asked by Francesco of Arezzo "to reveal
to him" the secrets of the Aeneid, which he had
mentioned in his epistle, Petrarch answered his
young friend that these explanations were, by
their very nature, doubtful and uncertain. How
could one be positive about the purpose of authors who wrote more than a thousand years
ago, or assert that they wished to say one thing
and not another? There may be, besides, several
meanings hidden in the same words, and others,
too, perhaps, of which the author in writing them
never dreamed. The principal thing is to discover
those that reveal moral truths, and this discovery
is at once easier and more useful than the precise meaning which the poet wished to express.
Taking advantage of this opportunity, Petrarch
offers to give his correspondents some of the explanations on which, he said, his mind had long
been fed. Aeneas represented to him the truly
virtuous man, eager for perfection; the devotion
of Achates expressed the precious companion-
ship of virtue and constant watchfulness. The forest they traverse in the first book is the image of
our life, full of gloomy shadows, of winding and
uncertain paths; it is barren and inhospitable,
inhabited by wild beasts and beset with difficulties and dangers of all kinds such as man en-
counters in his life. It has, nevertheless, its de-

ceptive charms: the freshness of the leaves, the
song of birds, the murmur of fountains—images
these of frail hopes and ephemeral pleasures and
illusions. As one advances the undergrowth becomes thicker; the approach of winter is like old
age, and the muddy roads are strewn with dead
branches stripped of every leaf. Venus appears
in the heart of this forest, which is much more
like Dante's than Virgil's. She represents sensual
pleasure, especially victorious in the middle of
the journey of life. If she has assumed the face
and form of a virgin, it is only the better to de-
ceive men, for did they see her as she really is,
they would flee from her with horror. Suddenly
the goddess disappears, to prove that nothing is
more fleeting and fugitive than the pleasure she
gives. She wears the garment of a huntress—does
she not hunt for souls? Through many long pages
Petrarch continued in such fashion to analyze a
multitude of details in the poem; and this letter, which is one of his longest, becomes a veri-
table handbook of allegorical interpretation. After reading it, one can understand the admiration
and anxiety which the talks of Petrarch excited
in good king Robert, who later confided to Boccaccio that he never would have thought there
was so much in Virgil.

These mediaeval dreams lasted much longer
than one dares to think. Torquato Tasso, when
he published his Rinaldo, in 1562, still thought

himself bound to precede it with a preface in which he gave a moral significance to every episode. Nay, more, in the century of Louis XIV, French writers of epic poems accepted the sway of allegory as a necessity in this form of literature; and Louis Racine, the son, taught that it was concealed in the whole of the Aeneid and in part of the Odyssey. We need therefore not be surprised to find these ideas in Petrarch, and we can only pity him for having fatigued his imagination in useless struggles with Virgil's meaning. The humanists of the quattrocento lingered long over the symbolist philosophy of the poet, trying to harmonize it with the doctrine of Plato, and darkening more and more the finest passages of the Aeneid with a thick mist of moral allegory. Petrarch had run the risk of reading Virgil all his life without understanding him. The poet's famous manuscript, annotated by himself, now in Milan, bears traces of a strange allegorical commentary which happily he soon renounced. He was saved from excess of symbolism by that exquisite literary sense which had early led him to choose his masters and his models from among the best Latin writers. He certainly read Virgil as a poet more frequently than he studied him as a moralist. Virgil's pathos touched him deeply, and he knew how to appreciate, for its beauty alone, many and many a verse, which he learned by heart. Preserved in his poet's memory, he found it again, happily transformed into Italian rime. Lastly, he hailed him, with patriotic pride, as the singer of the nation's childhood, and admired him with the sympathy of the writer who feels himself of the same race. No one will be surprised after this that he imitated Virgil in all his Latin work; and if this imitation, which he carried to excess in his Africa, exercised a decisive influence on the form of the Renaissance epic, there is no cause for regret. The fault of the Latin poets of the Renaissance was not in their imitating Virgil; they only knew how to imitate, and would certainly have gained nothing had they modelled themselves by preference on Homer. Their mistake lay rather in persisting so long to write in Latin, for the use of that language condemned them inevitably to an exclusive imitation of ancient models.

## CICERO

Like Virgil, Cicero was both model and friend to Petrarch. It was in consequence of the enthusiastic circulation of his work by the great Italian, that the fame of Cicero emerged from the conventional admiration which the Middle Ages had accorded him, and entered into the general culture of the modern mind. Henceforth and for long, to all who aspired to the title of man of letters he was held up as a model:

*Quest' è quel Marco Tullio, in cui si mostra*
*Chiaro quant' ha eloquenza e frutti e fiori.*

Petrarch invokes him in Latin with the same fervour he would have prayed to a saint of the Church: "O great Father of Roman eloquence! I am not alone in offering you my gratitude; with me are all those who deck themselves with the flowers of Latin speech. We sprinkle our meadows with water from your fountains; you are our guide; it is you who sustain and enlighten us! Whatever our talent for writing, we owe it to you. It is under your auspices we shall attain." Speak not to him of the Greeks! He knew nothing of Demosthenes, but he was convinced he could only claim a second place among orators, for Marcus Tullius towered over all! Plato perhaps equalled him in philosophy, but he could not surpass him. Thus Petrarch piled up favourable comparisons, which his ignorance of the Greeks rendered an easy task.

His worship was intelligent and sincere. As far back as his childhood the language of Cicero had always been an enchantment to him. "At that age, when I was unable to understand the meaning of the sentences, their sweet and sonorous sound sufficed to hold me, and all that I read or heard, which was not by Cicero, seemed harsh and dissonant to me" (quicquid aliud vel legerem, vel audirem, raucum mihi longeque disso-

109

num videretur). The scope and variety of work which Petrarch little by little discovered seemed to him still more wonderful. This it was, and not the outward form, which he endeavoured to copy in his master; since, far from paving the way for pure Ciceronians, he proclaimed, on the contrary, every author's right to form for himself an independent and characteristic style. It is evident that Petrarch wished to play the same part of philosophical and literary teacher that Cicero had played in Rome, adapting it to the needs of his own age. True, we do not hear him utter his ambition; but his eulogy of his illustrious guide has at times a personal accent which allows this to be divined. He knew that he was inevitably inferior on certain sides; but he did not despair of making a brave show in other respects. In oratory and statesmanship he could not hope to be another Cicero, although his speeches as an ambassador, his numerous letters of counsel to popes and emperors and Italian princes, brought him closer, as he thought, to his model. But he had something which Cicero lacked, for ancient testimony denies the gift of poetry to the great man. Later Salutati claimed far more for his master Petrarch in the comparison between the two, and placed him above all the ancients, without exception, for the universality of his knowledge and the versatility of his genius. Petrarch's vanity was continually urging him to compare himself

to Cicero. Whatever in their several lives and labours presented any analogy whatsoever, he drew attention to with much complacency. It was his own personal habits he was thinking of, when he showed how much the genius of Cicero owed to his withdrawal from affairs of state. All the famous villas that the Roman names recall those in which he himself had lived; and he could not help thinking that his books were written under the same conditions as the great didactic works of which he thus presents the picture: "Who can rightly describe the splendid leisure of the man, and describe his glorious solitude at Arpinum, at Cumae, at Pompeii, at Formiae and Tusculum? There did he draw up laws and defend the Academy; there he instructed the orator and expounded his conception of duty; there did he tell of the nature of the gods, uproot the errors of divination and prophecy, and determine the limits of good and evil; there again were uttered his magnificent exhortations to the study of philosophy. There he taught men the scorn of death, and the conquest of the ills of the body by patience, of the sorrow and sadness of the soul by reason. There did he show how the virtuous man has ever enough on which to live well and happily, and that virtue is enough for its own content. ... What others set forth in a dry and jejune way, he has described in rich and picturesque language, blending pleasure and profit, so that the majesty of the subject should not want for splendour and dignity in the words. And so his genius was inflamed by solitude." The hermit of Vaucluse and of Arquà was proud to think that he had fed his own genius at the same fire. Again and again he justified his bookish tastes by quoting those of Cicero; and in writing to his friends he was pleased to cite the example and the confessions of his master, to excuse the lack of all formality in his letters. In short, he constantly modelled himself on the Roman writer; and in his guileless vanity was always recalling this fact to his contemporaries and to posterity. It was a kind of affectionate veneration he felt for Cicero. Even more than in Virgil he found in him a brother of the craft, very famous, of course, yet with whom a certain intimacy was permissible. He wrote letters to him full of allusions to events in his life; and at times he pretended he had lived with him and been one of his friends (ex libris animum tuum novi, quem noscere mihi non aliter quam si tecum vixissem videor). Cicero, we know, has the gift of making us familiar with his surroundings; and after reading his letters we feel that we have been visiting the entire Roman society of his time. As the result of a portion of the correspondence which he discovered, Petrarch was the first of the moderns to enjoy this pleasure, and he gained therefrom a very correct idea of Cicero's character: "I have known him

as the consul vigilant for the safety of his country, and as the citizen always deeply attached to his native state. I leave to his keen mind the care of estimating his own position and the condition of the Republic. But, for my part, I cannot praise his soul, so changeable in friendship; nor his animosities, springing from trivial causes, which did him so much injury and served no worthy end; nor that barren and childish pleasure in disputation so unfitting to an aged philosopher." No one before Petrarch would have dreamed of writing such lines, which contain the first germ of the severities of modern criticism. During the Middle Ages, Cicero had been saved from such an estimate by the simplicity of his admirers and by their fragmentary acquaintance with his works. But the worship which his new admirer bore him, by its very reasonableness and reserve, only the more enhanced his fame.

It is impossible to exaggerate the importance in the history of literature of Petrarch's discovery of the collection of Cicero's letters. It was by this collection, which included the letters to Atticus and to Quintus, and the correspondence with Brutus, that our humanist became acquainted with the private life of the antique Roman world. He knew nothing of the existence of another collection, the Familiares, which Coluccio Salutati later discovered. Even his text of the letters to Atticus was, it appears, in a bad condition; but

from his studies of what he possessed he knew
how to draw excellent profit. There he found details of the lives of his beloved great men, which
elsewhere he might have searched for in vain;
and several of the letters enlightened him on unknown aspects of antiquity. Could he have recounted with such ease the life of Caesar, if Cicero's letters, even more than his speeches, had
not familiarized him with the Roman world of
his day, and with its chief personages? He would
hardly have attained to his remarkable insight
into the character of Cicero, if he had not learned
to know him in his private correspondence. After he had read his letters for the first time, he
addresses him as an old friend who had nothing
to hide from him: "I have eagerly read your letters which I searched for so long and found at
length where I least expected. I have heard you
say many things of yourself; I have listened to
your complaints and watched your changes of
mind, and, from having formerly known you as
the master of others, I have, O Marcus Tullius,
learned to know you as you were. . . . O ever
restless, anxious soul, or, that you may recognize
your own words, miserable and passionate old
man (o praeceps et calamitose senex), why did
you seek so many quarrels and stir up so much
useless hatred? Why did you abandon the calm
befitting your age, your condition, and your fortune? . . . Forgetful, alas, of your brother's coun-

sels and of your own wise maxims, you were like a traveller carrying a torch in the night, and it was for those that followed you that you lit the way in which you yourself fell miserably.... If good faith and love of liberty had inspired your conduct (as we should like to think of so great a man as you), how are we to explain your intimacy with Augustus? What answer can you give your dear Brutus when he says to you: 'If you like Octavius so much, you appear not to be fleeing from a master, but looking for a master who may be your friend.' ... O my friend! I pity your fate; but your numerous faults make me blush for you, and like this same Brutus, I am tempted to pay no attention to that philosophy of which you had a never-failing supply. Of what use to set one's self up as the master of others, when one turns a deaf ear to one's own teachings?" To those who reproached him (as did a certain ignorant and fanatic admirer of Cicero's, whom he met at Vicenza) for having attacked the great orator, Petrarch answered that he would not discuss the question with them until they had carefully read the collection of letters which had supplied him with his arguments. It is evident that he had correctly gauged the historic and moral value of this collection, of which modern criticism has formed an estimate corresponding with the general impression it left on its first reader.

Petrarch had carefully noted the titles and such fragments as ancient authors had preserved of several works of Cicero, lost to him as they are to us. The most famous of these was the De Gloria. He declared that he had owned it in his youth, and towards the end of his life he explained how he had lost it. This precious treasure, according to him, was in a book he had lent, and which he was never able to trace. I have elsewhere shown that the poet's memory was at fault, and that his imagination led him astray. By constant lamentations for his lost De Gloria, by thinking and talking of it to his friends, he persuaded himself that he had once read it in his lost manuscript. We have absolutely no reason for supposing that this treatise of Cicero existed in Petrarch's day. Petrarch's search for Ciceronian manuscripts, of which a large number were scattered in mediaeval libraries, will give the reader an idea of the attention which he devoted to all the ancient writers. He appears to have quickly aroused in his contemporaries a particular interest in Ciceronian research. The popes at Avignon, by his advice, made efforts to enrich the papal library in this direction. Clement VI requested him, through one of the clergy of his household, to come to Avignon and arrange the manuscripts of Cicero which were there. Later, Gregory XI took a keen interest in adding to the number. In 1374 he instructed a canon at Paris to let him know what

Ciceronian works were in the library of the Sorbonne, and to obtain for him good copies of such. He also addressed himself to Petrarch, who was then living at Padua, asking him if he were willing to lend the texts he was supposed to have discovered. To this last request we are indebted for a letter dated from Arquà, in which Petrarch describes to the pope's secretary his lifelong search. "You asked me to lend you whatever rare or unknown works of Cicero I may possess. I answered you that I had only the well-known ones, those, in fact, which belong to the sovereign pontiff, and I believe that mine are even fewer in number. I added only which was true, that I once had others, but have lost them, ... From my childhood, at an age when other children were studying Prosper or Aesop, I gave myself up entirely to Cicero, as much from a natural inclination as by the advice of my father, who had a great veneration for him. ... Later, I spared no pains to obtain his works, seeking them on every side. I had made many friends of all nationalities among the foreigners who frequented the household of the Colonna. When they were about to return to their country and questioned me as to whether I desired anything, I would ask them only for books, and especially the books of Cicero. I gave them a memorandum; laid stress on what I wanted, both by word of mouth and in writing. How often have I sent

Petrarch and his Masters letters and money for this, not only to Italy, where I was best known, but also to France and Germany, and as far as Spain and England. You will be surprised to learn that I have even sent to Greece." In his writings, he accords a particular mention to only a few of the large number of manuscripts he had collected in this way, among which, as a matter of course, there were several duplicates. The most ancient texts he possessed were a volume containing the treatise on Rhetoric, which he had read while studying law, and a book which he had inherited from his father. Either the one or the other contained the Tusculanes, which were familiar to him from his youth. A little later, Raimondo Soranzo gave him a manuscript of the De Oratore and the De Legibus. And soon every journey he made brought him in contact with Cicero: "I have never travelled for any length of time without discovering some unknown work of his. The very titles of some I had never heard of." Passing through Liège in 1333, he found there the Pro Archia and also another discourse, quite new to him, and he copied them on the spot. In 1350 he made them known to his Florentine friends, who used them to good purpose in perfecting their Latin style. "At your wish, I have brought back this discourse to my country," Petrarch wrote to them. "I found it long ago in the remotest place in Germany, when I was visiting that land with the eager curiosity

118

of youth; and now you have it and are reading
it, as I perceive from your letters which I have
just received."

His great Ciceronian discovery occurred in 1345.
At Verona he found the collection of the Letters
to Atticus, probably in the rich library belonging to the chapter; and as he could not make use
of a copyist, he himself transcribed the entire collection. He was in bad health at the time, but that
did not hinder his long work. It is easy to imagine with what love he accomplished the task.
He himself often spoke of it to friends: "Est mihi
volumen epistolarum eius ingens, quod ipse olim
manu propria, quia exemplar scriptoribus imper-
vium erat, scripsi, adversa tunc valetudine; sed
corporis incommodum et laborem operis mag-
nus amor et delectatio et habendi cupiditas vin-
cebant. Hunc librum, ut mihi semper ad manum
esset, in bibliothecae ostio posti innixum stare
solum vidisti." How we ought to bless the poet's
toil! His manuscript has, doubtless, perished; but
the original has been lost, too; and the text of
the collection is preserved to-day only through
a single copy made, after Petrarch's death, from
his transcript. Save for his devoted love to Cicero, this important work of antiquity would be
entirely unknown. He made the discovery at
Verona when his passion for Cicero was at its
hottest. Petrarch always travelled with one of his
books, or else he borrowed some from the book-

lovers of the countries he passed through; for all
of them possessed one portion or other of Cicero's vast works. One day, in 1344, detained at
Bologna by illness, and unable to set out on his
road, he cured himself by the perusal of De Finibus, which he picked out from the heap of volumes scattered about his bed.

Among the kindly purveyors to his classical
tastes, which his great reputation gained for him,
we owe a special mention to Lapo da Castigli-
onchio, the Florentine jurist, who himself seems
to have been very learned in things Ciceronian.
During his stay in Florence, in 1350, Petrarch was
taken to see him by Nelli, a common friend, and
he borrowed from him a manuscript which he
kept for over four years. His reason for delaying
to return it was that he had been unable to
discover a trustworthy copyist, and that he had
ended by doing the work himself (fatigatos hos
digitos et hunc exesum atque attritum calamum
ad opus expedio). This volume contained Cicero's
pleadings. Another manuscript from Lapo's library made Petrarch acquainted with his political discourses, and notably with the speeches
against Antony (the Philippics), which initiated
him into the Roman politics of Cicero's last days.
Since strangers showed such eagerness in min-
istering to the favourite taste of Petrarch, it is
not surprising to see his friends take pains to satisfy him. Boccaccio, the dearest of all, the great-

est book-lover, copied for him a manuscript containing passages from Cicero and Varro. Petrarch thanked him by sending him a parallel of the two writers into which he knew how to slip some delicate flattery: "The book is even dearer to me because it is written in your hand. This to my eyes places you between these two heroes of the Latin tongue. Let not your modesty blush at your presence among great men. You know how to admire intelligently what Antiquity, the mother of wisdom, has produced; but in your turn, you yourself, perhaps, will be admired by a posterity juster than the present age."

Thus, little by little, in the midst of his library, so rich in ancient books, there grew up an almost complete collection of the works of Cicero, which lacked but few of the manuscripts we possess to-day. This collection made by the chief representative of the most perfect Roman culture, placed at the disposal of the friends and disciples of Petrarch, was to influence the trend of thought from the very beginning of the Renaissance. This was assuredly one of the greatest services which the Father of Humanism could have rendered to the New Culture.

## THE END

OF THIS VOLUME
WITH TYPES & DECORATIONS
BY HERBERT P. HORNE
CCCIII COPIES WERE
PRINTED

OPTIMUM
VIX SATIS

BY D. B. UPDIKE
AT THE MERRYMOUNT PRESS
BOSTON MASSACHUSETTS
IN THE
MONTH OF DECEMBER
MDCCCCVII

155559